Life in a Small House in Crete

A Small House in Crete - (ISBN 9781
books) told the story of finding and th
accurately, the rebuilding of our small   ....se in a Cretan
village. The narrative ended when we eventually moved into
the house but this happened a few years ago and I wanted to
continue to record events as we started to live in the house.
This book is more a series of experiences rather than a
sequential narrative. Strangely, I am writing this in the midst
of a lockdown on international travel as a result of the
outbreak of the Covid 19 virus. So the reminiscing of life there
is an antidote to the grim stories at this time both here and all
around the world. The small village house is quietly sitting in
the village now enjoying the warm Crete spring awaiting our
return. There will come a time for rediscovering it, the Cretan
welcomes that we always enjoy and a parallel life to that in
northern Europe with the differences and contrasts that first
made the island attractive to us and made us want to spend
some of our time there.

I am very grateful to the people of Crete for their warm
welcome to strangers. I also can't express enough thanks for
the energy, imagination, enthusiasm and love given to us in
this project by my life partner S.

The colour images of the pictures in the book are available to
view at https://www.pinterest.es/geoffdendle/life-in-a-small-
house-in-crete/

CONTENTS

1 Questions

Once we had moved in there was the new responsibility of satisfying local curiosities about us. This ranged from enquiries on how long we were planning to stay in the house at a time to where we would shop. This was accompanied by recommendations, often conflicting ones.

There were also the direct questions such as 'How old are you ? Are you rich? How many houses do you have?" All asked without a trace of embarrassment.

Any purchase, however small would often have to pass a local informal inspection committee that usually sat opposite one of the kafenions at the top of the steps that led down to our house. The shopping was scrutinised by at least three of the 'yia-yias' and sometimes as many as five on a busy day. These were the same village ladies I had encountered some years before when clearing the house and had a similar mirror image scrutiny over what we were discarding. Acquisitions appeared to inspire similar levels of curiosity. Of course we didn't mind and both reflected how this was a much healthier way for the elderly to spend their later years rather than the 'shut in' ladies of a similar age in northern Europe. It also helped our slow acquisition of spoken greek although the vocabulary was mainly limited to listing the names of the various foodstuffs in our shopping bags. I have to confess there were days when I walked back to the house by another route which by-passed the 'committee' which involved walking down the main street and back up the alleyway below the house. But in the main the exchanges were enjoyable and helped establish us as new members, albeit temporary ones, of the village community.

It was also in part through these exchanges that we learnt the limitations of our greek language classes back in Sussex.

We had been warned by George, our Athens educated greek Cypriot language student that Cretans were different. We realised this when answering how we had travelled somewhere we answered 'by car' using the greek noun aftokinito - this was met with blank stares - I repeated the phrase this time aided by a mime of steering. 'AFTOCHINITO!" I was loudly instructed -the hard 'k' sound is sounded locally as a 'ch' softer sound.

This had led us into trouble earlier when hearing the word 'CHE' - like the legendary Cuban revolutionary. Our innocent request of a Cretan friend 'what is this word we are hearing CHE?" I thought you were learning greek ! It means 'AND' - we had been pronouncing it 'KAI' as mainland greeks did - so after four years of lessons we were could't say AND !!

The other way we thought to satisfy the ladies curiosity was to invite them to the house. This was offered on several occasions as we passed them sitting on their chairs at the top of the steps leading down to us, a distance of some thirty metres or so. The offer was always met with a shrug or a reply on 'avrio' meaning tomorrow and often used colloquially for 'not now but some point in the future, possibly.' At the end of a month's stay we had virtually given up and had packed for leaving the following day and put the bed out for the night and had walked up the steps to go into town for a last evening meal. The ladies or three of them were out on their chairs at the top of the steps ready for chatting with passers by and possibly some intense interrogation opportunities. They stopped us and in greek asked us where are you going ? To eat, in town.

When are you flying home. I was able to smugly reply ' avrio.' This caused some consternation and from what we could gather they were coming to see the house - now!

I went on ahead to tidy up and convert the bed back into a sofa, whilst the visiting party with a combined age likely to be in excess of 250 years slowly came down the steps. The windows were opened, seating arranged, glasses brought out and biscuits and crisps unwrapped. The visitors arrived and parked their walking sticks by the front door. Upon entering in unison they exclaimed 'orea' the popular greek adjective used for approval, meaning beautiful or very nice. Our decoration, a mixture of the old wood, stones and niches with modern lighting and bright colourful accents seemed to meet with their approval. We offered them drinks and snacks suggesting juice, coffee, wine or beer. All met with polite shakes of their heads until I suggested Coca Cola - which was speedily meet with 'Nai" and vigorous nods - yes, this was acceptable - perhaps the secret long life elixir for the elder ladies of the village. Once the drinks were consumed, quickly, there were curious glances cast upstairs and definite puzzlement over the glass panel in the upstairs floor. They all followed me upstairs pausing on the edge of the glass floor panel. When S. walked across it the act was met with much religious crossing of chests and a certain amount of tutting and the shaking of heads. Not aware of the greek for perfectly safe we just shrugged. After the upstairs room had been examined and approved of, apart from the glass floor, fingers were pointed at the spiral staircase. As the glass roof hatch was closed I was able to demonstrate one of the more unusual new features in the house. Flourishing the remote control I started the two electric motors that pushed up the large plate glass to the roof terrace. As it slowly and noisily raised the hatch to the open position there was a second flurry of the ladies crossing themselves - clearly further work of the devil.

The spiral staircase is not actually the easiest of accesses to the roof as the metal treads are quite narrow and you have to bob your head under the glass hatch as you step out onto the terrace. Anxiously I considered whether i should lead the way up or follow behind to break their fall if such a disaster should occur. Fortunately one of the Marias admitted defeat, patted her knee and returned to the safety of the sofa. But her two friends were not to be deterred and followed me to the roof terrace whereupon they declared the view to the sea to be 'Orea' and 'kala'. Not forgetting their stranded companion I was sent back down to get a camera to take a photo of Zographia and Maria 2 on the roof to show to Maria 1. I was relieved when we all were safely back downstairs as I am sure some spiral staircase roof disaster to a village yia-yia could force us to leave town. Refusals of more drinks were given and we eventually locked up and went to town for a belated supper.

2 The High Life

We had been told that access to the sea was a right in Greece and although hotels could discourage non residents from their grounds and sea front loungers many were happy for you to use the facilities for the price of buying a coffee or a drink. One of these resort hotels was in the next town and contained pools, bars, a seafront restaurant and and sunbathing terraces allowing swimming in deeper water as well as a small sandy beaches. It also had the benefit in the grounds of a rather surreal sculpture garden. It had been established in the 1990's apparently the legacy of an arts festival there.

Artworks included sculptures sticking out of the sea, a maze building, a huge Ariadne's thread ball, ten foot high racks of metallic sardines - an eccentric art treasure trove all in beautiful gardens between white painted small villa buildings some with private pools. We brazenly left the hire car in the residents car park and sauntered through the luxurious reception area into the grounds. I imagined that the secret is to look as if you are meant to be there and have found this is a universal passport to the most exclusive places. We sat under a shady canopy on a comfortable upholstered sofa and enjoyed iced coffees and the view. When the waitress asked us for our room number to settle the bill we asked if we could pay cash which was agreed and she confirmed the bar and restaurants were open to non residents as was the beach and facilities providing we were eating or ordering drinks - did we want towels for swimming? These were also available as were showers and bathroom facilities.

We agreed we had found a new dimension to our holidays. After a couple of hours lazing around we wandered up to the terraced restaurant overlooking the sea. Smartly dressed staff were bustling about and most tables were occupied although the diners were all fairly casually dressed as we were. One of the waiters approached, a smiling grey headed man who welcomed us and asked if we had just arrived. I explained that we were not hotel guests but could we still have table for lunch. The usual Cretan answer to many tentative questions was quickly given with a broad smile, "Of course!, but which hotel are you staying at?" -"Oh, no hotel, we have our own little house in a village nearby." He clapped his hands -"Fantastic, you have invested in our island - Bravo! Follow me." We were ushered by him to a table near the front overlooking the sea below behind the glass balustrade where he swiftly removed a reserved card -"will this suit you ?" Yes, very much -thanks you. The other diners to our

embarrassment were turning to look at these new arrivals who had been given the best table in the restaurant.
Once we were served with wine and bread and olives our new friend returned with menus for our orders but was more interested in chatting, where was our village, how long had we had the house, how many times a year did we visit - did work in England limit our visits - why not stay longer if we were retired? He was retiring the coming winter what hints did we have for retirement - well I could hardly recommend a house on a greek island - he probably already lived in one! A good lunch of sea food salads followed by fresh fruit and ice cream was followed by a laze on sun-beds and a swim in the clear, deep water off the terrace. We had found a new favourite place

for relaxing days and in subsequent visits to the island would often return.

3 Shopping

Living in the village allowed us to experience a particular aspect of village life.

We had already found that local traders plied their wares at the various regular markets on the island and we had learnt the regular days for each town where the same traders set up for the mornings business. In our town it was on Friday and as well as a number of fruit and vegetable stalls there were other businesses selling everything from local cheeses and honey to pop-up hardware stores and linen and clothing sellers. The range was from smallholders selling vegetables from their land to suppliers who also had shops in the towns so it was often rather disconcerting to go into a smart shop in the next town to recognise a familiar face that you remembered had sold you some tea towels at an earlier market. Still it all made for good business and the vegetables and fruit were very fresh, cheap and of good quality. The regular markets had another advantage: I once bought a pair of cotton jeans without trying them on. At home there was a realisation that they were 'aspirational' and did not appear to be accurately labelled for size. The following day we went to the next town for their market and to track down 'Mr Trousers' as we had christened him who was happy to exchange them for a roomier size. Needless to say no receipt was required.

In the village during our first stay at the house we were surprised one morning to hear tannoy music moving through the narrow village streets, followed by shouting of repeated greek words that sounded like the words for shoes and socks. Sure enough when we followed the sound up to the top of our street there was a pick up van with a tannoy on the roof of the cab and a flat bed behind it full of boxed and unboxed pairs of shoes, boots and sandals. The van was already partly surrounded by a number of ladies of the village some already trying on the latest shoes, others with wrapped purchases handing over their euros. It was an advanced Cretan form of on-line shopping with the advantage of a 'try before you buy' offer. Over time we recognised the various offerings so we were able to buy kilos of oranges for pressing fresh orange juice at the end of our street as well as other goodies, We were

11

wrong footed on one occasion when a rush to the van after not recognising the loud, spoken offering to find the sales were limited to snails and raki, the local spirit. We resisted whilst acknowledging that to some this might constitute the ingredients for a 'good night in.'

The markets in town were also socially important and the bars and restaurants in town around the harbour near the site of the market always enjoyed the busiest morning of the week as the shoppers refreshed themselves with frappes, juices and coffee afterwards whilst exchanging details of successful purchases. Over the years the market moved location from one of the back streets one road back from the main square, the road narrow enough to have welcome shading by tarpaulins screens stretched between the stalls. A location popular with the restaurant owners nearby. Then some genius moved it some several hundred metres up the hill on the site of the unfinished by-pass road. This was short-lived, unpopular and at our next visit it had moved back down the hill for a few years until it was moved nearer the beach on the site of the old children's playground. It has stayed here with the old gravel strewn playground having been modernised and re-sited on soft artifice play surface next to the beach promenade. The resurfacing demonstrating some nod to modern health and safety sensibilities not always witnessed on the island (see Cretan scaffolding and driving discipline!)

We usually drive down to the market and search for a parking space as it's one of the busiest days in town. One of the best buys is a large bouquet of fresh vegetable, fronds of fennel, greens, kale and celery bundled together. The local hard and soft cheeses are always tempting particularly as the sales technique involves generous tasty samples. The shopping is followed by an iced coffee in our favourite bar which will be crowded with other shoppers before taking the precious supplies back to the house. Often the shopping would have to pass inspection by the village ladies from their chairs who we discovered went to the market themselves but at a much earlier time. We had discovered this fact accidentally one evening after innocently replying to a question from one of the Marias whether we would be going to the market the next day.

The 'Yes, of course -can we get you anything?"
The reply of -" No - I will come with you -meet me outside my house at seven."
"SEVEN O'CLOCK?" - 'Yes -" she mentioned "kala" which seemed to indicate this was necessary so as not to miss "the good stuff"
We set the alarm for about two hours before we were usually breakfasting and called at the house for the drive down. En route we recognised Iorgi the church warden who doubled as the bellringer in the largest of the three small churches in the village. He stuck his his arm out and I just managed to avoid maiming him by slamming the brakes on. He opened the back door and got in the back next to Maria. After some good mornings Maria started some instructions to me which I interpreted as instructions to turn off the air conditioning. I recognised the greek for cold and as it was accompanied by a shivering mime I concluded this was for Iorgi's benefit as she had been happy until he got in. Iorgi was wearing his summer wardrobe of a tweed jacket, V neck jumper and collar and tie and as it was only in the low twenties we didn't want him to get a chill. We asked where we should take him - the market? No -the church which was on the way so it should be easy but a near accident almost occurred when our elderly hitchhiker opened the back door prematurely and seemed to be climbing out before I had stopped! No damage was done and with a wave Iorgo crossed the road to the church accompanied by honking from two motorcyclists he had totally disregarded in his ecumenical hurry. We tried to ask Maria whether he expected a lift back to the village but this was only met with a shrug of indifference. On a later market visit with Maria we learned first hand that these were not always seen to be return trips as we lost sight of Maria in the market and after a decent interval I drove up the hill expecting to see her but she was not en route or at home. So I drove back to town only to spot her sitting in the passenger seat of a neighbours car being driven up the hill. There was still much to learn about local customs.

The market was surprisingly busy, in all honesty we had not realised it started this early. We normally planned our weekly visit to end with elevenses coffees. Maria seemed to know

everyone which wasn't surprising as the customers mostly
were contemporaries of hers but there were also a few faces
we recognised as owners of the smaller restaurants and cafes
presumably shopping before opening their businesses.
Several on recognising us asked why we were out so early -
'just bringing down a neighbour' was my answer which was
met with a knowing smile. This was another disadvantage- as
they were out shopping they had not opened their cafes or
bars yet so we couldn't have our second morning coffee out -
at 7.30 ! Maria announced she had all her shopping and it was
time to go home.
After driving her up the hill and arguing with her about me
carrying her shopping - an argument which I lost, we said our
goodbyes - thanking us she pressed a large chunk of wrapped
cheese into my hand -it had been quite a morning and it wasn't
yet 8 o'clock. Maria went off home and to open her one room
kafenion next door - one of the many octogenarian cafe owners
on the island.

4 Livestock

The village house was seen very much as a holiday home and we knew that because of the size limitations and commitments back home and for similar reasons we had not unreasonably assumed we would not have any pets or livestock at the village house. For good and bad reasons this turned out not to be the case. On one of the first days in the finished house I was trying to locate a strange metallic sound inside the house. I had reasonably assumed this was something to do with the architect's high tech installations. I examined in turn the motor for the roof hatch plus it's UPS box (an uninterruptible power supply gadget with its constant eerie blue led and allegedly installed in case we entertained sufficient guests on the roof terrace to require the hatch to be closed and a simultaneous power cut would have stranded all 8 or 9 of us up there!) Then I listened to the fuse box near the front door - not that either. The water system had an electric pump but that was also silent so not that. Then I remembered that the led lighting strip that was one of the nicer features and lit the gap between the two floors was served by some high tech transformer resembling or possibly made from a chrome box style cheese grater- that wasn't the culprit either.
Suddenly the buzzing increased in volume as a huge flying beetle flew out of a large knot hole in one of the ceiling beams in the upstairs room, it orbited the room several times and thankfully exited the house through the open window. It was one of the largest insects I had ever seen and I spent the next half hour filling the hole and locating and filling similar ones in the other beams. Still the mystery of the source of the noise had been solved. I would like to say this was the scariest visitor to the house but that would not be true.
My next scare was on an early visit where I decided I needed to familiarise myself with the spaces under the metal hatches in the ground floor. One was the septic tank which I wisely left alone, the second was the reserve water tank which somehow magically provided us with water in the event of a mains water failure. The tanks had water in it and some complex pipe and float arrangement that was beyond my rudimentary plumbing expertise so I replaced the hatch. The last hatch covered a

fairly deep hole containing some electrics connected to a large cylindrical pump on top of which sat a tiny white insect that I recognised as a scorpion, I rapidly replaced the hatch. As with much of our experience in Crete we relied on local knowledge for information. This was always very readily given but often it did little to clarify things as within the space of minutes two people could confidently provide totally contradictory information. Unfortunately, in this case my casual request whether I should worry about a scorpion in the house -"it was only a tiny white one" was confidently and unanimously met with the sucking of teeth from several acquaintances and advice that it should be dealt with and that they were by far the most dangerous and would require medical attention for any sting. Somewhat chastened and armed with a hammer, torch and an insect spray the next morning found me cautiously removing the hatch. Of the scary but tiny monster there was no sign and thankfully in the years since we have never seen another one either in the house or anywhere else -quite a relief.

Our next encounter was quite early on in our occupation. One of our neighbours kept chickens which was nice to have a rural chorus of the hens and the occasional cockerel wake up call. Being a mediterranean creature his wake up call wasn't too early for us, certainly some time after dawn and the hens provided benefits to us via the mezes in the owners kafenion with small plates of sliced, hard boiled eggs provided when drinks were bought. The drawback though was that any fowl keeping is usually an attraction to mice after any spilt grain. We had spotted the occasional mouse dropping in the street but so far we hadn't experienced any small, furry uninvited guests in the house and we were very careful not to leave any unwrapped food around or unwashed crockery. The visit when it came was rather dramatic. A scratching in the ceiling above us in the corner of the room while we were sitting on the sofa was quickly followed by a large brown furry creature complete with a long tail running down the wall! It disappeared through the gap between the two floors and scurried on down into the wet room below the stairs. As I was the only member of the household not clutching my head between my knees and

16

shouting "It's a RAT - a RAT" I nervously went down stairs to investigate.

No sign of the rodent in the wet room - but some noise from the cupboard under the stairs where the water heater was. So nervously prodding the door open with a broom I quickly established that our new pet had returned upstairs and S's scream of "THE RAT !" seemed to definitely confirm this. It had returned, run up the wall and left through the corner he had arrived from.

We slept fitfully having placed a phone call to our favourite Albanian builder Ianni with a request for an urgent visit the next day.

Iannni arrived just after nine o'clock the next morning accompanied by one of his men who we had met before on an earlier building job they had completed for us. As Ianni didn't have his interpreter son Elvis with him the description of the work required was described by us with a mixture of poor Greek, English and mime. Our pointing out of the hole and mimed description of the intruder was met with amusement but also Iannis "No problem " verbal agreement. We had discovered there appeared to be no word for Rat in greek but the term 'Megalos pondecos' - large mouse was used somewhat euphemistically. We followed Ianni around the house as he carefully examined the house for all potential entrances for the pondecos - Megalos or micro. The house structure complicated things as the metal framework in each corner ran through the house from ground level to the roof on the first floor and seemed to be masking some holes through the stonework as well as in the roof where they met the ceiling. Ianni assured us it was "no problem" and after pointing out some other small gaps above one of the window lintels Ianni said his goodbyes after announcing 'Avrio" - tomorrow and indicated nine o'clock. The next morning Ianni and Polychroni arrived at nine and started mixing mortar in the street outside and after a few hours a smile and a thumbs up indicated the job was done. We drank coffees together and paid the agreed price in euros but Ianni said "tonight - at seven, Maritsa kafenion in town - beer!"

Thankfully, we have never seen a rat in the house again but we did meet Ianni that evening for beers in town. He was there already and ordered beers for us, smiled and said "Elvis-here soon." This would make conversation easier as Elvis was fluent in Albanian, Greek and English but before he arrived we raised glasses and said "Yamas" -then he said "in Albania - Geezer" or that's what it sounded like as we repeated it. Then he asked "English?" - we said "Cheers" Ianni repeated "Cheese" with a broad smile - "no, Cheers!" Ianni raised his glass again -"Cheese."

Further conversation was rescued by the arrival of Elvis, Ianni's eighteen year old son and our interpreter. A bottle of beer was ordered for Elvis and he was proudly toasted by his Dad with a raised glass and an enthusiastic but somewhat bewildering to Elvis, cry of "Cheese!"

The celebrations continued with Ianni ordering food -Elvis explained they often shared a snack here after work. In short order a large platter arrive with a fork for each of us. It's an omelette explained Elvis. We asked what was in it - "Eggs and Chips" explained Elvis. I am sure the original Elvis would have approved. "Is it good?" asked Elvis -"Yes, thanks - let us pay." "No need - there will be no charge - I supply the eggs -I have sixty chickens."

So the Rat episode ended with a new experience - Chip omelette with Albanian friends. The island continued to surprise us.

5 More Livestock

When discussing the 'pondecos visit' with friends in the village whilst admitting the connection with chickens there was a more obscure and unexpected explanation. "More people are keeping dogs as pets in the village - this scares away the martens." This was news to us. These are pine martens and they come into the village - "yes - to steal eggs and eat the pondecos - they come at night" We were learning new things about village life daily.
One moonlit night returning to the village after supper out we spotted a creature jumping from roof to roof and it's long bushy tail confirmed to our more knowledgable friends that this was a marten. A few days later there was a scratching noise on our roof terrace and through the small roof light window we spotted a creature creeping across our terrace onto the roof. With its tail it looked to be over three foot long and seemed much larger than the village cats who were usually rather small but apparently co-existed with them. They still must be rare visitors to the village and normally nocturnal and those have been our only sightings of the marten.

Our next visitors are much more frequent and generally more welcome - these are the village cats. You are always aware of the cats in Greece and Crete is no different. The combination of a kind climate, livestock in the villages and generous humans putting out scraps seems to provide a secure livelihood. This certainly seemed to be the case in our village where a number of the same cats have lived for over ten years at least to our knowledge. The local cat charity also runs a sterilisation service so that the population levels seem more sustainable. Since before we actually occupied the house we had come to recognise a few of the feline residents and once we had occupied the house they made their presence known on our visits. If they hadn't arrived within half an hour of our arrival then the next day once we had placed our chairs in the alleyway outside they would appear and occupy the chairs at least several times a day for the period of our stay. The two most recognisable were Jazzy, a healthy looking mixed coloured tabby and ginger cat and Ginger a smaller, nervous

and scraggier specimen - so nervous that we can rarely touch him/her / it ? Jazzy was the less timid of the pair and would happily come in the house or jump up on a lap. We were convinced she lived with someone as she seemed well fed and healthy but local knowledge described her as being 'owned by the whole village' and the abundance of empty accessible buildings meant that shelter was not a problem. Ginger was often seen with minor wounds and eye problems but he seemed a survivor and we concluded he was a small tomcat and was sustaining fighting wounds. On returning to the village when we had been out we often had to walk with care as one or both of them weaved in front and behind us anxious for their next measure of hospitality. Initially it was only saucers of milk or some scrap of cheese or cold meat from a lunch but it wasn't long before cat food was added to any shopping expedition and if it was Maria in the town mini market who served us her "I see you have a cat now - are you moving here?" had to be met with - "no still holidays we have a share in the village cat." This was confirmed one evening when walking out we passed our Jazzy and Ginger eating out of saucers on the terrace of one of the houses below us that we knew was owned by a French family. We laughed and said they were doing well as we had already fed them - " Yes", they explained "we call them Isabella and Isabella 2" - so the cats had aliases, as well as several suppers! Who knew.
Initially we thought this feeding was a northern European soft-heartedness and there was some discussion that the cats still need to be hungry some of the time to suppress the local "pondecos population" but sightings of some of the elderly village ladies putting out scraps for the cats confirmed they were of a similar mind to us. We once asked what happens in the winter - are they still fed? This was confirmed but it was also stated that the village cats had been known to make their way down to the harbour to be fed fish scraps from the fishing boats. It was less than a mile away so quite possible and all the more believable after a sight we saw in one of the nearby towns.

We were sitting one morning drinking iced coffees under the shade in one of Neapolis cafes in the wide road in the town centre. It was more of a square really as it was wide enough for double parking and still enough room for the local buses to execute a u-turn. Watching the double parking was one of the entertainments on offer here as a trapped driver would return, wait for a few minutes or longer before putting his hand on the horn to summon the owner of the offending vehicle trapping him. All of this was conducted in a good natured way and I guess the drivers were known to each other and later the trapper would become the entrapped. Opposite the cafe we noticed one piece of the road with a few cones in it which was being ignored by the double parkers and we also realised that between the cones in the road sat a couple of cats. In the next ten minutes they were joined by several other cats who didn't seem to interact with one another but just patiently sat and waited. The mystery was solved by the arrival of several lady shoppers carrying shopping bags shortly before at midday accompanied by hooting and loudspeaker calls of 'PSARI'-fish, fish - the pick up from the Nicos fish restaurant in our town arrived in the square. These Cretan cats could tell the time and as we were told the fish sale was weekly; they also had calendar knowledge - impressive!

Other livestock in the village were gecko lizards seen running up walls and often in houses but I can only recall seeing one in our house that came in through an open window and went out the same way in seconds. At times of the year one or more of the crickets temporarily moved into the village from the olive groves nearby but their chorus was fairly short lived as they were either picked off by a bird or became a temporary plaything for one of the cats. So far the sheep and goats grazing the hillside bordering the village had resisted the temptations of a more urban life, maybe the abundance of barbecues had dissuaded them from venturing nearer.

6 Ianni

I have mentioned Ianni before and the help he had given us in 'mouse, (and rat) proofing' the house. He had come to us by way of recommendation from one of the kafenion owners in the village and the first piece of work was the completion of a narrow juliette balcony outside the small double doors on the first floor. We had spotted a similar one to the sort we had in mind on a newly renovated stone house in the village and local enquiries had led us to contact with Ianni and his student son and interpreter, Elvis. By sign language and with the help of Elvis we had previously discussed this balcony, agreed a price and arranged that we would have the work carried out during our next visit to the island. So a couple of days into the next stay having shopped, remade acquaintances, acclimatised ourselves to the warmer weather and pace of life in the village we both agreed we felt resilient enough to allow builders into the house.

We phoned Ianni and in rudimentary greek I explained we were in the house and ready for the works - at least that is what I thought I had said. Similarly I believed Ianni said he would arrive the following Monday at eight, at least that is what I thought he had said!

Sure enough the following Monday we heard some movement in our alleyway outside and as we had taken the precaution of rising early we were dressed and just finishing our breakfast of yoghurt, fruit and coffee. A smiling Ianni was accompanied by two other workers both bigger than him, he was small and slim but seemed very strong judging by his handshake and the large pieces of scaffolding he had carried down the steps on his shoulder. We were introduced to the taller of his colleagues as Polychronis (meaning multi coloured/) who smiled broadly and crushed my hand with his handshake. His compatriot seemed to be called Borgia or Bourgos we were never quite sure but no matter they all busied themselves assembling tools and materials in the narrow alleyway. I offered coffees which was accepted but Ianni came into the house and indicated he wanted an electric plug which I showed him. After the coffee he showed me the three large wooden supports that would hold the balcony and then via sign language and pointing to a

24

large 'kango' hammer covered his ears, shook his head and pointed to us and indicated the steering of a car followed by the term ' kafenion in Schisma'. I understood there was going to be some noise and dust and he was advising us to clear off into town to have a coffee and avoid this. It sounded good advice. At this point I thought it would be prudent to confirm the price that had been agreed with him several months before at the end of our previous stay in the house. This gave me the opportunity to use one of my frequent greek phrases - 'signome - poso kane' excuse me - how much? He confirmed by writing on the pavement with a small stone - 500 euros. Great, we subsequently discover during other work commissions with Ianni this seemed to be his fixed price quote to us and the secret was to establish in our own minds that enough work was included to justify his price so for example when later on we asked him to render the walls of the terrace he agreed to continue the rendering part way down the wall which faced the sea and the prevailing winds and where we had noticed some damp coming through the stonework. The best thing about Ianni was that he did what was asked, to a good standard, on time and at the agreed price and he was nice to have around the house. That morning we took his advice - he suggested closing the shutters and locking the house up after feeding an electricity socket through the small bathroom window. Come back this afternoon he suggested.

As we walked through the village up to the road behind the main church where the hire car was parked, a distance of several hundred metres we could still hear the thud of the kango hammer. In fact I swear I could hear it above the car engine as we drove down the hill to the town. We returned a few hours later after a more restful morning than we imagined the village was enjoying.

In our absence the team had bashed three large holes below the french doors on the first floor and had inserted three thick beams, broader than my hand width and sticking out from the house by a foot or so. Ianni indicated that they were fixed and cemented in and they would leave for the day to let it settle before returning the next morning to construct the balcony. I should explain that the balcony had been part of the original planning application but we had not proceeded with the construction as part of keeping costs down and trying to bring to a conclusion the somewhat protracted building works. (The full story is in my earlier 'A Small House in Crete')

For the house restoration and planning and building consents we had always agreed with the architect that the works must be legal. We had discovered in the process that local planning regulations stipulated that balconies should not project further than 10% of the width of the street and our street or alleyway was only three metres wide; I had often joked that i could stretch and touch both sides simultaneously, not strictly true but close! This allowed us a 30 centimetre balcony. Our sticking to legalities was borne from hearing horror stories of buildings needing to be demolished, boundary disputes and other difficult situations that we were anxious to avoid. Certainly we wouldn't be seating four people round a table out there - we had the alleyway and the roof terrace for that.

Thinking of sitting around a table led us to consider offering the workers lunch the next day. We had shopped at one of the local markets two days earlier and the fridge and larder was well-stocked. Why not? There were few opportunities for home entertaining as it was more normal to meet with friends out at a restaurant and share a meal. Often this was a literal sharing of a meal with the convention being to order numerous plates and everyone to dive in and sample dishes on their own plates. Fried courgettes, tomatoes dishes, fava beans, black eyed beans in vinegar, fried haloumi, stuffed vine leaves, grilled meats, cheese pies, spinach pies, horta (season greens-boiled), octopus and calamari, snails even! All served with local bread, oil and olives. We had many of these or the ingredients so the next morning we asked Ianni if they would have lunch at home with us. It would give us a chance to test entertaining inside the small house as the last two occasions we gave some friends a meal we had set out the table and four chairs outside in the alleyway. Ianni's workbench and tools in the street meant we would be inside.

While the craftsman were constructing the balcony in the street we went to town to get some last minute ingredients including some of that morning's freshly baked bread from the bakers. There would be some limited cooking but we lacked an oven at this stage and had one small ceramic induction hob that would take one large pan or two small ones at one time. In the heat of the June day it was unlikely we would want hot food so any of the cooked ingredients could be prepared one at a time before meal time. Progress outside was going well; the woodwork frame, floorboards and handrail had been fitted and Ianni explained it would be primed with the final top coats put on the next day. I think he said he would return by himself for this as his guys were off at other work. So the lunch was to be a farewell to them. After we admired the finished balcony from below we assembled in the downstairs room which now had a dining table as well as two extra chairs around the table opposite the storage benches. The house suddenly seemed full but one at a time Ianni and his guys washed their hands in the next door wet room and once the lunch party assembled I offered cold beers all round which was well received.

The spread of food seemed to be appreciated and everyone tucked in. Conversation was initially difficult until it was established that Borgia understood English and could speak some, certainly to a higher standard than our Greek and non-existent Albanian. Conversation initially focused on the food and it was mostly confined to appreciative noises and smiles. Then talk moved onto building - the fact our house was stone, not concrete was considered to be good and comments were passed on the beneficial coolness in the Cretan climate. It turned out the Borgia was initially from Bulgaria which gave me a conversational link as I had once holidayed there in the 1970's and described it as a beautiful country and remembered Varna and an impressive aquarium there, he seemed pleased that someone appreciated his homeland. Though it was acknowledged that Crete was a great country - plenty of building work!

The next day the top coat of grey paint was applied to match the existing external woodwork with the job completion celebrated with cold beer and home made honey sponge cake brought to us by Ianni's wife who had come up with him that morning to be shown the 'pretty house.' Judging by her polite but slightly mystified reaction it may have been described to her as a 'pretty unusual house'. The glass floor and 'shock ' multicoloured tiling in the wet room were both met with hand on mouth gasps and once she recovered from the motorised hatch the panoramic view from the small roof terrace was met with the usual '*Orea*' beautiful.

7 Hatch fix

One of the more radical features of the house was the electrically powered glass hatch that gave access to the roof terrace. This consisted of two motorised arms that apparently were the type used to power garage doors. The mechanism was linked to a black box with a small blue light that housed a battery pack to provide an uninterruptible power supply as back up in the event of a power cut to the mains supply. The raising and lowering of the heavy plate glass hatch was operated by a small remote control unit. It had operated perfectly for our first few visits to the house until one morning it failed to move. I tried the spare remote controller but that was the same. Looking at the 'magic black box' more closely I realised the normal blue led wasn't lit. A trip downstairs confirmed the trip switch for that circuit was still ok so did it mean that both motors had failed? Since we had moved in the builders merchants in town had become one of my more frequent destinations so I would go there to seek advice having taken several photos of the possible culprits on my phone. Arriving in the shop which stocked everything from boat chandler and fishing tackle to bathroom fittings, tools, paints and a full range of building materials. You could just wander among the aisles for inspiration or go directly to the sales desk or wait to be ambushed by one of the staff or either of the two brothers who own the business. Perfect english could be spoken and pleasantries were always exchanged - I had even been offered a cake or a biscuit if a large box was being shared on the counter.
The standard greeting, if I looked too confused browsing the well-stocked shelves was 'how can we help you - what are you trying to do at your house?'
I displayed the photos on my phone and explained we had a glass hatch to the roof with an electric mechanism that seemed to have failed. "You have electricity in the house?" "You have checked the fuse?" Confirmation of both of these served to deepen the mystery. "Can you be at home after two today

when we close -I will come to the house, where is it?" I did the usual set of directions using the recognisable landmarks of the main church, the kafenions and named neighbours. "I will find you - look out for me -I will come by moped." I did the reminder about the set of steps on both footpath routes to the house. "No problem -I will park at the kafenion." Shortly after two o'clock we heard the distant buzz of a moped coming up the hill. We had a good vantage point from the roof terrace of the road from town up to the village as well as the zig zag road from the hills above the village. A few minutes later a smiling Stavros was at the door armed with a tool roll. I showed him the fuse box and then led him upstairs to show him where the magic black box sat on a wall bracket next to the spiral stairs. The two arms of the roof raising mechanism sat stationary above the box and remained in that state despite several pressings on the remote control. Stavros leant over from the spiral stairs and reached the back of the black box. He pulled one wired plug, then a second. Then he pushed one into the other and pressed the remote control. The hatch motors whirled in their normal fashion and Stavros smiled in triumph.

You need to by-pass the back up battery it has failed. I will take it to the shop and see if it holds a charge. Come to the shop in tomorrow and I will let you know. It seemed an easy solution, much easier than I had expected and another example of the learning process of the workings of our little house.

Sure enough the next day the problem was sorted out. Stavros showed me the magic black box split open and the battery pack inside. "I have tried to recharge it but it's not having it - it is kaput - but no problem it is the same type as we sell for boats and lamps used by the fishermen. Here is a new one, it is 15 euros - I will dispose of the old one." It was a typical example of the readiness to help that we were regularly encountering on the island. I was reminded of this later that month when driving through the next town and noticing for the first time a sign outside a restaurant. " TAVERNA STAVROS - NO PROBLEM" So unbeknown to our new technical helper I have since described visits to the builders merchants as 'going to see Stavros - No Problem.'

8 House Layout

The design and renovation of the house is described more fully in the previously published 'A Small house in Crete' but I have since realised that I could have included a floor plan and a 3 D sketch of the house. I have put this right by including it here. The house itself is a basic box with the windows and door all on the 'street-side' or more correctly on the alleyway which slopes slightly downwards as you face the front of the house. The front face of the house apart from the grey painted front door has four deep window openings, one for each floor with double wooden shutters and matching small double opening windows. The third was a tiny square window into the wet room on the ground floor. The last opening was upstairs and was a pair of double opening glass doors with wooden shutters and after one of Ianni's 'improvements'; now opened onto a narrow wooden balcony with a sideways view over the bottom of the village and the olive groves to the town and coast below with the distant mountains visible across the bay.

At the roof level the pitched tiles only occupy half the roof space with the back half comprising a walled 'cut out' for the terrace. This is accessed from the top room up a spiral staircase then onto the small terrace via the raised glass roof hatch.

Inside, after coming through the front door, a door on the right leads into the wet room that is partially under the stairs. On the right hand side of the main room the wall curves around to give space for the wet room. A cut out in this houses the fridge freezer with shelves for a larder above. These two are disguised by recycled shutter doors salvaged from the house in

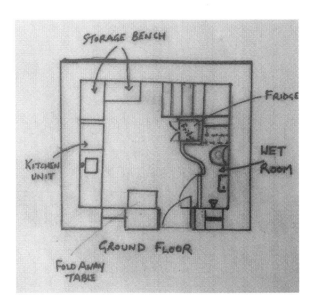

its original state before rebuilding. They are painted in 'mediterranean turquoise.'

We have painted the curved wall a bright orange which reflects the light coming down through the building from the large plate glass panel in the floor of the room upstairs. On the left is the kitchen bench with the sink unit. The original bench in the finished house has been replaced by a flat pack mini Ikea kitchen in an industrial style with stainless steel worktops. The 'cooking facilities' comprising a stand alone halogen hob and a microwave/electric mini oven/ grill combined. They are stored in the cupboard of the unit from which they occasionally emerge, mainly due to our enthusiastic patronage of the many and varied eating places on the island. We do like to support the local economy! To the side of this is an L shaped arrangements of cushion covered bench/ lidded storage boxes where our clothes are kept. Scattered around the walls are a series of niches let into the thick stone walls, all with down lights. In the larger ones we have fitted plate glass shelves and on here are coloured glasses, china and storage jars all chosen for their decorative qualities making the niches looking like display items in a kitchen or china shop.

A set of stairs in the back right hand corner of the room leads up and around the back of the curved orange wall. On a small half landing as the stairs turn right we have fixed some wall storage for shoes and books. The stair backs have plate glass risers which allows some light into the wet room below.

The upstairs room has a split level ceiling height. It is lower at the back of the house below the roof terrace and higher to the front of the house to allow a row of roof light window bringing light from the roof terrace. The large plate glass hatch atop the metal spiral staircase brings more diffused light into the house, down into the kitchen through the glass door panel and through the metal perforated treads of the spiral stairs into the stairwell below. Two more deep niches in one wall provided useful storage with another bench box used to store bedding and linen. The furnishings were completed with a comfortable sofa bed, two wall desks and two armchairs made of clear perspex next to a small perspex trolley/table all chosen to create a sense of space. The view through the glazed panel in the floor help create a feeling of spaciousness in what really was a small house. A wall hung air-con unit was tucked away on the wall behind the spiral stairs next to the hydraulic mechanism for raising the hatch which kept this 21st century technology in one place but slightly out of place with the ancient stone walls and wooden beams.

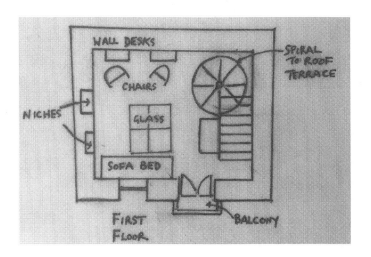

The small roof terrace normally has a pair of director style wooden and canvas folding chairs with a ledge around the retaining wall for placing glasses or cups. Of course the best feature of the roof terrace was the view, a 360 degree one taking in the village, the surrounding mountains and the town and coast with even higher mountains in the distance way across the lagoon and the bay beyond it.The other omission from the first book mentioned by readers is that I didn't give any indication of costs. This may have been deliberate on my part but to go a little towards satisfying their curiosity I will tell you firstly, it cost more to renovate than the initial purchase. The costs were incurred over the several years that the work took and because of this we were subject to the vagaries of the exchange rates of the pound to the euro. This provided a variation of up to some thirty percent between the most favourable and detrimental rate. The house was bought originally for the price in Britain of a premium family car if that helps give some gauge of the expense. The transaction costs, fees and renovation costs were approximately twice as much again so it was a sizeable investment for us but less than the cost of an average house extension in the UK these days

9 The 1 euro lunch

To more modest matters of finance, we had always found meals out in the many restaurants and cafes to be good value particularly given the cheery service and the freshness of the local ingredients. It is fair to say that prices had increased relatively after Greece had joined the euro and consequent fluctuations of the exchange rate sometimes meant that a good dinner in a restaurant in the resort with a waterside location can be a similar price to the UK, with the exception of the local wine which was much better value and if chilled, perfectly acceptable. Our concept of good value was soon to be rocked by the '1 Euro Lunch.'

On one of our drives out to Ierapetra on the south coast after a morning in the shops there I suggested stopping on our way home in one of the villages between there and our village. The village we chose is called Episkopi and in follow up reading I have learned that like many on the island it is suggested it was founded in Minoan times around 2500 BC. The area still depends on agriculture for its livelihood, particularly olive oil production from the surrounding olive groves and you are just as likely to see a local worker drive into town on tractor as in a car. As we parked the car in what we supposed was the village centre we saw a brown Greek tourism sign on the opposite side of the road. Crossing over, cautiously watching out for speeding tractors which seem to travel everywhere at a fixed, and not slow, speed. I was once told this was to do with the limitations of hand controlled throttles but I am doubtful about this. It's more likely to do with the casual attitude to danger generally prevalent in the farming industry - just a thought. Arriving safely onto the pavement we were surprised to see a small domed Byzantine styled church squatting below road level. Strangely it looked at the same time ancient but also in good condition with fresh smooth rendering to the walls. The gated entrance was padlocked but the notice board in Greek and English gave its date as 961 AD ! Over a thousand years old and looking like new. Further reading described renovation works carried out several years earlier which explained things. We promised to return and see the interior when open but now for a cooling drink. We found a small cafe with a shaded veranda and ordered a local bottled beer to be shared between us. It came with two glasses and a small dish of chopped tomatoes and olives in oil with cubes of the dried bread, dakos in a small pile in the centre. Very welcome we thought. We were asked by the lady proprietor where we had come from and upon hearing the name of our village she seemed to express surprise although we knew we were less than an hour's drive away. Returning inside to the kitchen we heard the noises of further for preparation and assumed we were witnessing the preparations for her lunch time rush of local tractor drivers but no - she returned with a larger dish of salad with four hot cheese and spinach pies sitting on the side. To our more cynical northern European eyes this looked like some Cretan high pressure salesmanship but we were hungry and it looked good and there was no rush so hungrily we polished it off. Her concern for our sustenance on our onward journey was not entirely reassured as the empty plate was whisked away and replied with a plate of grapes and a small flask of raki, the local grape spirit, no doubt to help steel my driving nerves against errant tractors on the journey home. Our appetites very much sated I asked for the bill - and a small hand written note was handed with a single line on it. Is it a nine or eleven - it can't be a seven —that is always crossed and it can't be one ! I queried with one of my frequently used greek phrases -"Poso Kane?" How much? The lady held up one finger 'Ena euro" It was one euro! For the first time in my life I left a tip of several hundred percent of the bill. We were all pleased - and it has passed into our memory as Episkopi the home of the ONE EURO lunch, maybe more memorable than a new thousand year   old church.

10 Thripti

The roof terrace was a favourite sitting place but due to the heat it was only usable for us at certain times of the day. We had discussed putting some kind of shade up similar to some of the other houses in the village. The drawback was the loss of the 360 degree view which due to the way the village sloped away just below us gave an 'on top off the world' feeling which we were reluctant to lose. The terrace was usable for breakfast unless the day was particularly hot. A sun shade umbrella could be used up there in the day but the middle of the day was usually too hot for us. The space came into its own from early evening onwards when the sun started dropping below the mountain behind us bringing some welcome shade. At this time we could watch the cars and mopeds on the road below and above us. The owners of the smallholdings below us would come to feed the livestock and water the crops. The village taverna would open with enticing smells. Below in the bay the last of the tourist boats from the old leper island would return to their moorings for the night. Small fishing boats would cross the lagoon and white sailed cruising yachts would anchor in the bay for the night. In the bay outside the lagoon the occasional cruse ship would sail by in the distance leaving Crete for another island. Later the lights would come on both in the village and down below in the town where coloured neons favoured by some of the bars and restaurants gave a pretty twinkling kaleidoscope of colour. Once it was completely dark the sky was large enough that shooting stars or satellite trails were visible helped by the clarity of the warm night air.
One night at sitting on the terrace at dusk we noticed on the mountains in the distance, very high up, a trail of car lights towards the summit. Surely there's not a road up there ? Getting the binoculars and a map by torchlight we worked out it must be Thripti. The spot height on the map showed a height of almost 5000 feet. Taller than any mountain in the Uk! Looking through the binoculars it seemed the cars had parked and it looked like a torchlit procession to a church, although we couldn't be sure because of the distance.

It became an aspirational destination. Enquiries locally suggested it was accessible to drive there although opinion was divided on the best route and several were offered. Also offered was the question as to whether we had a four wheel drive vehicle. When I said no only a small ordinary hire car the helpful reply of "No matter, that should be ok and if not - it's not your car!" Not exactly reassuring.

Nevertheless, one morning armed with our best map and making sure we had a bottle of water in the car we set out to follow what on paper looked the best route. Leaving sea level at the coast we started climbing on a main road that was known to us as the route to Sitia ,the largest town to the eastern end of the island. The road climbed for some miles and across the bay we could see our town and the smaller mountains on the north coast. In a village that seemed to be the point where the route on the map headed south and showed a small winding grey minor road line that ended in Thripti. It felt like a minor adventure but it turned out to be short-lived as the steep, winding road which started with an old but solid tarmac surface soon deteriorated to a gritty unsurfaced track full of ruts and potholes and given that we had seen a road sign giving the distance as some 20 kilometres further ! Thwarted we cautiously executed a U-turn praying that some local farmer in a hurry for their lunch would not broadside us in mid manoeuvre.

A refreshing drink at the taverna back in the village on the main route brought fresh information. 'You want to go up to Thripti - not in that car over there" -our hire car was pointed at. 'You need to use the road off the Ierapetra road, longer but easier in your car." We finished our drinks and decided to drive home and try another day.

We had temporarily abandoned our Thripti expedition until Ianni came to the house to quote for another 'improvement' project, some rendering of the walls on the roof terrace where we suspected the stone and mortar construction was allowing some water down the wall. While talking on the roof I spotted a glass reflection, probably from a car, up on the distant mountain. Through the usual process of broken english and greek, supported by mime, I asked Ianni if he had ever driven up to Thripti and was it an easy drive from the Ierapetra road. His reply was his usual confident 'No problem' and indicated that he could drive us up there on Sunday in his large 4 x 4 Japanese pick up. It was generous offer but one we decided that we would not take him up on for several reasons. One - Ianni worked long hours and Sunday was probably his family day as it was for many people on the island when tourists would share the restaurants with large local multi-generational family groups eating late and lavish Sunday lunches. Two - several hours in the car would be quite a stretch for conversation with Ianni without a shared language. Lastly, Ianni had lived in Greece for many years and although I had very limited knowledge of the general standards of driving in Albania and of his own standard of driving it was possible he may have adopted the Cretan driving style which meant that you would not limit yourself to just smoking whilst driving if there was chance to hold your mobile in the other hand whilst still waving to anyone you knew on your journey. So we declined but decided we must make the journey before our next encounter with Ianni as to refuse twice may look rude. Later that week on a clear late morning we set off to conquer the summit! We were heading to Thripti. We had a clear day with no commitments, not unusually, and had watched the mountains across the bay since breakfast and after a few hours the peak had emerged from the clouds that often shrouded the mountain tops. The drive south took us past Aghios Nicholas and along the coast road past a number of bays next to the turquoise waters. There was no rush so we stopped and had a cooling drink at coastal cafe, cool under the canopies that gave welcome shade to the tables. Setting off again we turned onto the Ierapetra road and the mountain destination soared high above us on the left side of the road. We could see the deep cleft of the Ha gorge, one of the largest on the island and looking pretty inaccessible because of the amount of stone scree at the bottom of it. Nearing Episkopi (the village location of the legendary 1 euro lunch,) we spotted the road sign to Thripti - only 22 kilometres. The road was a good tarmac surface and initially straight until you went through a hairpin bend and doubled back on yourself as it climbed upwards. I foolishly commented that this seemed to be ok and then met a speeding pick up driven in the middle of the road on the next hairpin bend. We moved more cautiously after that, all the time climbing with the olive trees giving way to rougher bushes and then to our surprise a forest of pine trees which continued for some minutes. I later read that this pine forest is one of the largest on the island but had suffered a large forest fire in the late 1980's. It had certainly recovered since as the density meant I had put on the car headlights and lived in hope that any oncoming Cretan 4 x 4 drivers would be exercising the same precautions - though this was not a confident view based on experience.

In fact our most surreal road experience had occurred the previous week when driving to a monastery. It was one that we regularly visited in the mountains behind our village which had a pretty courtyard garden with ponds that were significantly cooler than the land, lower down nearer the coast. That afternoon as we neared the monastery I became aware of an old pick up we had previously seen parked at the monastery - it was in the middle of the road coming towards us - forcing me to swerve onto the grass verge to avoid a certain head on collision. As it went past us I saw that the driver was a monk who seemed to have white opaque milky eyes -no pupils! Had we witnessed a blind monk driving to the next village guided not by sight but the hand of god- who knows? I was tempted to turn round and follow him back to the village to confirm what we had seen -(and he hadn't) but fear of meeting him returning as he may have only been on a short suicidal test drive. It was an early and extreme encounter with the now fashionable, in some circles, practice of going for a drive to test your eyesight! On subsequent return visits to the monastery I have intended asking anyone I would meet there whether a blind brother was one of their number and if so why was he driving around. Sadly the monastery has always been deserted although the garden is always well tended. Strange but not untypical of unusual island encounters.

The journey to Thripti was completed without incident although it was hard to describe it as an enjoyable drive. The road seemed to get narrower and the drops to the side of it more precipitous with few parts of it having any fences or crash barriers. The views had for most of the journey been distant and spectacular but my fear of meeting another vehicle and concentrating on the sharp bends had prevented me from appreciating it. I had consoled myself with thinking I would be able to appreciating it at the top and I could relax.

Unfortunately, it didn't quite work out that way as for the last few hundred metres to Thripti we realised we had driven into the clouds. Upon reaching what appeared to be the centre of the village we parked the car next to the only other vehicle we could see - a red painted water bowser with a flat tyre. Perhaps a precaution against a re-occurrence of the 1987 fires there? The other realisation was that it was bloomin' freezing, relatively; the temperature seemed to have dropped some twenty degrees. As some consolation we saw a building in the corner of the square with a light in the window and a taverna sign above the door and promisingly, smoke coming from the chimney. We needed no encouragement so went inside where the three people: a lady wearing a thick cardigan and two men both clad in winter wear of flannel shirts, boots and thick gilet type jackets, one even wore a wooly hat. They were sitting around a blazing fire in a large inglenook style fireplace. It was hard to believe that we had left home in shorts and sandals and a temperature at sea level on the digital thermometer outside the town pharmacy of 31 degrees.
We were offered a table and ordered drinks. I hoped the beer was warm.
Looking out of the window it appeared to be getting darker even though it was mid afternoon. Of course, as is customary we were brought some mezes to eat with the drinks. These were some small cheese pies accompanied by a mix of warm fried vegetables out of a pan cooking over the open fire and very welcome it was too. After we paid it was too cold outside the way we were dressed to sight see so we got into the car for the scary ride back down vowing to return another day. At home we often look across the bay to Thripti in the mountains and have noted that the summit is invariably clad in a thick mist.
Perhaps the torchlight procession we had witnessed was to keep their hands warm !

45

11 Accountants and tax

Under Greek law permanent residents are required to submit an annual tax return and this process is usually conducted through their accountant. After the completion of the house we were told that this arrangement also applies to foreign nationals in Greece who own property. Initially, it was arranged through the accountant of the architects who had offices in the next town and submitted our annual nil return of income in Greece and billed us for the service. We are always anxious to simplify matters and place any business locally where it makes sense so one day in our local favourite cafe bar conversation turned to whether there was a local accountant who could perform the service for us and who would speak English and we could communicate with from England. "Of course - there is my uncle and his son who works with him and they both live here in town, just up the road. Here is his number. Tell him I sent you and you are friends of mine." I must explain that on the island personal recommendations, often for relatives businesses are the norm, rather like 'the landlord down the pub, in England' before many pubs became managed and part of national chains.

On phoning the number later in the week we arranged a meeting for 11 a.m the following morning. My son will be present - he studied in Britain he can help translate, his English is better than mine. We were then given directions to the office on the ground floor of his house in town, the directions were in perfect English. The next morning we arrived at large white painted house with a pretty front garden and shuttered windows and we were shown into a large office room with a tiled floor and several desks with a computer on each one. The walls were lined with cupboards and bookcases, it all looked very business-like. We shook hands with a distinguished gentleman probably close to my age and he introduced his son who was to work with him since returning from his studies abroad.

"How can we help you - I understand you have a house here"
I went through the usual description of the house and where it was in the village, with no house number, in the street with no name but between and below the two kafenions.

"I think I know it. Who sold it to you and how long ago?"
After I provided the details as well as the sale price - always a
point of interest. It was agreed that yes he knew the family
although he was not sure he had seen the particular house -
"Families here often own a number of houses" without telling
me how many he owned nor how much they cost but it seemed
rude to ask.
I handed over our previous tax return receipts and explained
that we wanted to use a local accountant and a friend had
recommended him. "Ah yes, he is a relative by marriage a
second or third cousin - many of us in town are related.
I have had some bad experiences with people from away but
we need new customers and as you are friends of friends let's
see what we can do."
We had heard rumours and had read about new taxes to be
applied to raise revenues since the financial crisis and the
bailout of the greek economy. One tax, later withdrawn,
suggested that foreign home owners without greek citizenship
were required to deposit an amount of money into a greek
bank account annually with the amount varying with the value
of their house, ownership of a swimming pool, car or a boat.
The annual amount started at over £10,000 euros but bizarrely
could be withdrawn and sent back to the 'home country' once a
certificate from the bank had been produced confirming the
deposit. The logic of this process escaped us so we had chosen
to ignore it, somewhat nervously! We had always said we
would attempt to do everything legally with the house and this
included paying taxes. So we asked whether this bank transfer
arrangement still applied. "Ah no, it was seen as unworkable
and would not actually raise any revenue while taking up
unnecessary efforts for Greek civil servants."
For clarity I asked what taxes and obligations they could advise
us that we would need to meet.
"Firstly, what square metre has been declared to the
authorities. It will be shown on your electricity bill."
I shuffled our small file of receipts and officialdom papers and
pulled out our latest electricity bill and handed it over.
"Ah good, I can see you house has been transferred from the
construction tariff to a residential tariff. This means the
authorities are satisfied your works have been signed off by

the inspector and therefore in the eyes of the authorities it is a legal building with no taxes relating to the works outstanding"
Phew! Friends and already indicated this but it was comforting to have a more official confirmation.
"It says here the house is only 40 square metres - tell me how big is it?"
I replied "It's 40 square metres and that includes the roof terrace."
Look of amazement passed over both their faces - the Accountant junior said
"But nobody declares the true size - everyone gives a reduced amount to suppress the taxes based on size!"
I said "they can come and measure it if they want and that will confirm the size"
The rather panicked reply was -" No, No - they wouldn't do that - is that what would happen in your country - Oh No that would cause all sorts of problems - it would undermine trust! Still I am not sure they will believe 40 - it's too small!"
"Well I will suggest they come and measure."
This caused Accountant senior and Accountant junior to go into a long and complicated conversation in Greek which only concluded when the phone was picked up and a further conversation in rapid and loud greek was instigated.
"My father is speaking to the tax office."
This went on for what seemed like too long and I fully expected the outcome would be an army of tax inspectors descending on the town armed with tape measures and clipboards and resulting in us being hounded out of town by an angry mob of local home owners. The loud exchange finished after some ten minutes, though our anxiety made it seem as if it lasted longer than that.
"The office say that because you have no car, boat or swimming pool here and your house seems so small you don't owe any further taxes this year. If you have no income in Crete for the rest of the year we will complete a nil tax return for you next year. Come back in the spring and we will arrange it all.
"That all seems very good but what do we owe you?"
The surprising reply was - "Nothing. Come back next year and we'll complete the return for you. It will be less than 100 euros."

We had a new accountant looking after us - I wondered if I could engage him to argue with the UK Inland Revenue on our behalf?

12 Kitchen

When the house was finished we had asked for simple bench kitchen to house the sink and to prepare food on. We had always seen this as temporary solution and we wanted to live for a while in the house before we decided what we would need in the house in the longer term. When making a life change there is usually a mismatch between how you think things will be and how they actually turn out. At home we regularly had the house full of visitors for meals and unconsciously we seemed to have assumed something similar in this house. Though I think the suggestion was always there that it would be simpler local fare and lots of cold drinks and to this end we had stocked the kitchen with enough crockery, cutlery and glasses to supply up to a dozen people. In reality a dozen people in the house would be standing shoulder to shoulder or pushing one another off the roof terrace, though we could overflow into the street- a technique often used by villagers and bars and restaurants. We could always tell when the taverna in the village was expecting a large party or hosting music night as dozens of extra chairs and small tables all magically appeared from somewhere and blocked the main village street for the evening. At least ours was not a through alleyway!

In truth after the initial visitors inspecting the finished house it was rare that we entertained there beyond offering drinks and a small plate of mezes and most communal eating took place by meeting up at one of the many excellent eateries in the nearby towns and villages.

Nevertheless the 'kitchen unit' consisting of a simple worktop housing the sink with a storage shelf below was never seen as the permanent kitchen solution and after exploring several options we discovered that Ikea provided for us the perfect solution. A range of stylish units in black wood and stainless steel available as flatpack with just the right amount of cupboard and drawer storage for our needs. So we bought them and were then left with the dilemma of finding a way to get them from the UK to the island almost 2000 miles away. Up until this time we had either bought large items on the island or confined 'imports' from the uk to items that could be carried in a large suitcase and this we had tested to the limit with two flat pack metal wall cupboard/desk units brought ever even before the house was complete. This was not an option for the kitchen units so we started searching the internet for courier type services from the UK to Crete. Often in life a solution happily presents itself and happily this occurred again. An old university friend who had been the first person to visit the house with us before we had 'sealed the deal' and bought it was also building a holiday home on the island. Although we were good friends he had chosen a plot several hours drive away in the south of the island near Lato the archeological site and not far from Matala the resort popularised by Joni Mitchell in the 1960's. One day the phone rang at home in Sussex and Dave was calling, I am planning next month to drive a van overland to Crete to take some things out and wondered whether you want anything taken as well as there should be some room. Had to find a tactful way of asking how much room he was offering as we were, in our requirements, talking literally of the kitchen sink - together with the rest of the kitchen!

Once I had provided the sizes of the flat pack kitchen boxes Dave had agreed that there should be room so a few weeks later found us meeting in a Kent pub garden off the A2 on his route to the Channel tunnel. His vehicle already looked full but with a repacking exercise our heavy packages were placed on the floor so they wouldn't damage his expensive looking bikes and cycling accessories. A sensible precaution once I was told the wheels and tyres alone cost several hundred percent more than our kitchen. Once it was all repacked we wished him a safe journey and wondered when we would next to see our kitchen.

It was later the same year that we found ourselves in Crete at the same time as Dave and we were able to arrange the collection of the boxes after measuring the luggage area of the hire car to ensure it wasn't a wasted journey. We set off for the south - a journey that we estimated would take us two to three hours. The day was warm and the sun bright with the first part of the journey travelling west along the National road towards the capital, Heraklion. This part of the journey was very familiar to us as it was the route between the house and the airport. It was relatively busy with speeding taxis, minibuses and coaches as well as the normal traffic of private cars, pick-ups and vans. Some of the route was now dual carriageway which I found safer than the two lane roads on which the protocol was the car being overtaken was expected to pull over onto the hard shoulder to allow overtaking. One of the main dangers was finding something parked there! The other danger was the impatience of the overtaker who would push up to within inches of the rear of you to force you across. This was the typical behaviour of the large Mercedes taxis but they were not alone in this aggressive approach - it didn't make for a relaxing morning's drive. The traffic thinned out after the airport and became even quieter once we passed the first junction of the National road into the capital and headed south. The road climbed and fell following the contours of the surrounding mountains.

The vegetation changed and we began to see large vineyards of low growing vines covering the hillsides either side of the road. As we travelled further south this gave way to the more normal cover of olive groves as well as some small fields like market gardening with mixed crops. Large birds of prey circled high overhead occasionally swooping down into the undergrowth for their quarries. After travelling for over two hours we were in need of a break so I was pleased to see signs for Mires one of the larger towns on the route so I suggested a stop for a mid morning coffee. The town was interesting and very different from the more tourist orientated coastal towns.The heat further south gave a dusty atmosphere to the streets and this was accentuated by the large numbers of tractors and other agricultural vehicles parked in the main street, no doubt contributing to the supply of local dust. We found a cafe with a shaded veranda and ordered two iced coffees which were very welcome. The main road seemed well served with agricultural suppliers and builders merchant leaving little doubt as to the main sources of local employment. Refreshed we drove on out of town and found that the scenery changed again to sandy covered soil between the olive groves and quite large numbers of sheep and goats grazing of sheltering in the shade under cover of the trees. Another three quarters of an hour found us driving into our friends village and we could see his new white villa style house on the ridge above. From the narrow road above the house the land fell away and in the distance we could see the south coast, the turquoise sea beyond which and out of sight lay Africa.

I reminisced that we would have expressed surprise many years ago as twenty year old students we would be meeting as homeowners on a greek island. Dave welcomed us with cold drinks and reintroduced us to his sons who were staying with him. We sat on the terrace overlooking his garden which he admitted was proving to be a maintenance liability and complained that his planting had proved something of a magnet to the local goat population. We sympathised but reflected our lack of grounds to our house allowed us to avoid similar worries but agreed that his house position had beautiful views to the snow capped mountains to the north.

We arranged to lunch at a beach taverna a few minutes drive away on the coast but first of all we collected the flat pack kitchen boxes from his storeroom and established that they would fit in the hire car which was a relief.

Lunch was the usual sociable sharing experience of a table full of delicious vegetable and seafood dishes and after a refreshing coffee back at the house we were saying our goodbyes and driving our kitchen in a more laden car back home to our village on the north coast. The late afternoon was a little cooler and we were driving with the sun at our backs which was more restful on the eyes and we made the return journey without a stop. Parking the car in the narrow village street just above the house and briefly blocking the through route the large boxes were manhandled down the steps and into the house. A project for another day.

The construction of the units seemed as straight forward as most Ikea projects. I knew it would be a mixture of carefully following the instructions, looking for the pieces you thought had been missed out but in fact had rolled across the room and been obscured by existing furniture; swearing - once you realised the part that had been particularly tricky to assemble was, having looked at the instructions again and more carefully having wiped the coffee ring off the vital picture - had been assembled inside out, upside down, counterclockwise or all of the above! Normally, I had rather masochistically enjoyed such challenges and had some experience with the allen key and hammer approach. The main difference with this project was attempting it in a day-time temperature of 30 degrees plus. I had taken the precaution of firing up the air condition unit to it's lowest setting, an aspirational 16 degrees, closing the shutters to the outside heat and placing some large bottles of cooling drinks in the fridge as well as topping up the ice cube trays. Of course the job was not straight forward - stage 1 meant removing the existing kitchen unit which required disconnecting the plumbing and then us both struggling to get the unit out of the front door; a task made more difficult until we realised that it must have been built inside the house and could only be taken out in pieces so the hammer was necessary. Once there was clear space further progress was delayed by the blowing of the electricity fuses after I had tentatively prodded some taped up wires in a niche behind where the unit had been. The fuse blowing had belatedly confirmed they had been live !

A lucky escape ! Which then led to an investigation in the mysterious fuse and circuit breaker box to find which one to remove or switch off to make things safe. Safety first suggested turning all the electricity off and opening the shutters for light - which then let in hot air.

Half an hour passed while we identified the fuses and labelled the switch box with the circuits each one covered - a task I had meant to do in the previous months and cursed that the electrician or architect had not done this although if it had been completed in greek, not unreasonably, it probably wouldn't have helped me. So and hour had passed, there was a clear work space, no-one had been electrocuted and the errant wires were safely tidied away in junction box. On the down side we had already consumed half of the cold drinks supply and I had sweated enough to need a shower but as I had turned the water mains off for the plumbing work to be completed this was not an option.

The kitchen units were unwrapped and the pieces covered the floor of the kitchen. I really hoped the packs were complete as nipping up the road to the nearest Ikea would involve a trip by plane or ferry to Athens on the mainland. With crossed fingers and a sweating brow the frame for the units began to take shape. The first storage unit was assembled in half an hour and we were very pleased with it. The double unit housing the sink was next and I now felt we were on a roll. The excitement over the near electrocution had subsided and the air conditioning unit seemed to be doing its job . A break for an iced coffee maintained energy levels and the prospect of a cold beer, shower and supper out didn't seem too distant. The most scary task that I had now to complete was cutting a hole in the stainless steel work surface to take the mixer tap. An earlier trip to the wonderful builder's merchants in the town had provided me with cutting tool that I had been assured would complete the task. When I had asked whether I should use it by hand or fix to a power drill I was met with a horrified expression and given a very thorough talking to on the folly of this. Stavros described to me that it would have to be done slowly and delicately, 'like surgery' otherwise the consequences could be disastrous! Thus it was with some trepidation and a certain amount of cynicism that I approached the task not really believing that hand pressure was going to cut through what seemed to be quite heavy duty stainless steel. Of course, as usual he was right, a perfect hole was cut and the tap fitted through it and before long the water was turned back on and we were admiring our new mini kitchen. It really seemed a pity to spoil it by messing it up with a meal and washing up so after a well deserved celebratory cooling glass and showers we set of for supper out in one of our favourite restaurants; smugly basking in a sense of achievement after half a day of to us, hard work.

13 Plumbing

The plumbing system in the house had always been something of a mystery and to our mind rather more complex than necessary. The kitchen sink and wet room all functioned well and the house also had an outside tap near the front door and another outside tap on the roof terrace. The water system had a back up storage tank that we were advised was necessary in case the mains supply went off and there was an electric pump to increase the pressure. On occasions when coming back to the house after several months away the pumped system failed to work and the pump had to be 'persuaded' to work again by opening up the floor hatch, the one were I had previously encountered the scorpion, pressing a reset button, by torchlight, hoping not to attract the curiosity of any resident scorpions. This usually, happened after arriving at night after a long journey and not in the best frame of mind for trouble shooting!

A conversation with a neighbour suggested this pumped system was unnecessary as the water pressure in the village was much improved in recent years and this was confirmed by using the outdoor tap which didn't use the pump. So can we find a good local plumber to sort this out? George was recommended by Kenny, a friend who phoned him and explained roughly what wanted and it was arranged that I would meet him by the church and bring him down to the house as he was not familiar with the village and could not use the usual directions based on the two kafenions and the taverna. The next day at the appointed time the rendezvous happened and George was early in his red van as described. We walked down to the house and I asked him where he lived as he was unfamiliar with the village. He named a village a mere ten minutes away by car but remembering that our house lacked a number or street name it would seem churlish to be critical of his lack of local knowledge. Using sign language, minimal Greek, (knowing at least the expressions for water and no water) along with demonstrating the water pressure from the mains using the outside tap I think we reached a mutual understanding of the work required. There

was a worrying moment when George having removed the tiled metal hatch covers in the floor was subjected to my best impression of a scorpion that may or may not be living there. I think he understood and without any knowledge of what personal liability a householder assumed for poisoning a visitor to their home even if the poisoning was committed by a third party and the third party was an insect -it really didn't bear contemplation. Fortunately, George stood upright unscathed and with some relief I quickly put the hatches back down.
We agreed mostly through pointing the parts of the installation to be retained and the parts to be removed so we were only left to agree the cost and date for the work. He said (or at least we both thought he said) tomorrow morning, all for fifty euros. This seemed very acceptable and we shook dusty hands and he left. Experiences with the use of 'avrio' i.e. tomorrow or as we have found 'not today' but some future date it was some relief that we opened the door to George the next morning carrying a large bag of plumbing equipment. After refusing coffee he got straight down to work. Good as his word within a couple of hours the hatches were back down. All the taps and the showers were working at a good pressure, even the one on the roof. The street outside had a tangle of copper pipework that was no longer required as well as a massive electric pump the size of a commercial fire extinguisher. George then demonstrated the water pressure in the simplified system which was working fine - even from the tap on the roof terrace. I asked George whether the pump and the copper was of any use to him and this produced a broad smile - this was pronounced as 'Kala' and when we paid him with a tip for good service he seemed even happier. The outcome was very satisfactory and we now had a plumbing system in the house that I understood with the bonus of a couple of storage boxes in the floor under the hatches that I could keep things as long as they didn't object to sharing the space with the elusive white scorpions!

14 Kenny Rogers

The revival of beard growing in the 21st century has been a source of mystery to me. We were able to blame the Beatles amongst others for the popularity of face hair 'back in my day' but I am not sure who to blame in this century. Nevertheless I was intrigued a few years back to hear of a website which celebrated the trend among 'older gents' to sport grey or white beards on the apparently popular web-site "Men who look like Kenny Rogers." On this site people could post photos of men who they believed look like Kenny Rogers and in fact many of them did resemble the bearded country and western singer, (and some frankly despite having silver hair and beards did not.) Being of a grey hair persuasion myself but no longer sporting a beard maybe worrying I might look like Kenny or even worse Dr Harold Shipman - it's a fine dividing line. I just stored the fact of the website away until one sunny morning in the square at Neapoli whilst we were quietly enjoying watching life go by and enjoying cold frappes (iced coffees) ....Suddenly out of nowhere and from a side road into our field of vision passed a motorbike ridden by either Kenny Rogers himself or the best contender ever for "Men Who Look Like Kenny Rogers." Of course he was gone before I could get out a camera or get the camera app on my phone but hey this was a small town despite being the regional capital- he would be back, hopefully soon. After half an hour of lazily soaking up the atmosphere we gave up hope of sighting Kenny again and vowed to keep our eyes open, and cameras ready, on future visits to this town which we had previously thought of as the town that had more than it's fair share of monks and where the cats know the time and days of the week.
Future regular visits we usually punctuated by statements of "I wonder if we'll spot Kenny today"
The next sighting was around a year later but this time he arrived in town in pick up truck - definitely a Kenny Rogers mode of transport but as we were again sitting amongst others, maybe relatives of his, it seemed inappropriate to hold up a camera to get him in shot as he sat in the cab on the other side of the square. I'll wait until he gets out and hopefully he'll walk this way and holding the camera discreetly

at waist level I can unobtrusively 'shoot from the hip' as it were. Sadly, we were thwarted again as a second man joined him in the truck and they drove off with 'Kenny's face obscured by the passengers head. Damn, this was clearly not an easy quest but we wouldn't give up.

I am not sure how long it was before the next sighting but just like the others it was an unexpected encounter.

Neapoli was always a relaxed place to go. It was a small town that could be approached by two interesting routes if you decided, as we usually did, to avoid the excitement of the new national road with the hurly burly of coaches, lorries and the bullying tactics of the taxis rushing back and forth between the airport and the coastal resorts. One route was over the mountains north of our village and through several large villages and then dropping down past a cultivated plateau down into Neapoli. On this road there was an intriguing part of the road raised above the surrounding fields and shaded on both sides by an avenue of mature trees, more like a french road than anything usually found on the island.

The other drive was up from the coast along the original old road that skirted the hills above a deep gorge for some of the way until it cut down to run between irrigated olive groves with their networks of snaking plastic pipes. It went through a couple of small villages that we had visited occasionally for some memorable lunches that were usually better value than the already very reasonable prices in our own coastal town. As we approached the town nestling below surrounding high hills, mountains really, we passed a row of old stone windmills built in row climbing up the slope towards the new national road. We had visited one at the time we were planning our house as our architect had planned the conversion of it into a gallery/shop. It was an interesting space, narrow with curved walls at one end and split level inside the thick stone walls.

I have mentioned the double and treble parking regime in the town square here before and it does provide gentle entertainment from a vantage point of one of the cafes on the shady side of the square. There are a number of small local shops in the town and we have used them for shopping ranging from shoes, electrical goods, paint and beautiful old fashioned ledger books that S. has used for her garden journals. The bookshop owner always seems to derive a certain amount of amusement when we return annually and ask for one of them to be lifted down from one of his top shelves which can only be reached by a step ladder which has to be brought out from a storeroom at the rear. I am sure that like everywhere else Cretan business accounts are now on Sage software or something similar and we are buying up the last of his stocks. The book is brought down, carefully examined and dusted, (which suggests this is not a fast moving stock item.) The shop is always empty of customers and the proprietor, a gentleman of advanced years is pleased to see us again. The thick, heavy book with it's substantial cover which almost feels as solid as wood, and the multi coloured moire patterned page edging is a particular purchase and all for 12 euros!

In the back streets of the town many of the buildings stand empty some boarded up, some lacking roofs and having trees or shrubs rooted inside over the years. The county court and some regional government functions are still here but it seems like a town with a past with more recent economic activities having migrated to the coastal towns. The schools and the nearby monastery and seminary together with the courts give a certain amount of activity at particular times of the day and there is always great opportunities for just sitting with a cooling drink under the shade in cafe and watch the world go by- with the bonus of perhaps sighting Kenny and even getting photographic evidence this time.

The next encounter was a chance one as we walked down one of the back streets in the town. This was always interesting as we had discovered on one visit a workshop of a lyra maker, the traditional stringed instrument used in Cretan music. The craftsman kindly spent some quarter of an hour showing us how he painstakingly built the instruments, bending and shaping the curved wooden soundbox even though at the outset I was at pains to explain we weren't in the market for a purchase and neither of us could even play any musical instrument. In another road on one of our first visits to the town some ten years previously we discovered the 'Shepherd Shop' - seriously, fully stocked with all the equipment required for full time shepherding, apart from the sheep and dogs. At the time we owned an Irish Wolfhound back in England and often had difficulty finding a sizeable collar for him so we were delighted to find a range of long leather collars of large sizes - for goats? Other stock included a lethal range of knives and shears, collar bells, leather boots and everything the gourmet shepherd would need for cheese making. Recently some good friends bought me a birthday present of a cheese making kit so thank you Daryl and Martin, I know here I may be able to buy extra stocks of equipment should I want to up my production. Although our greek classes were deficient in giving us much vocabulary used by cheese makers, back to the standby of sign language I guess. Still we were now an established customer having made some purchases there - one large collar and one copper sheep/goat bell. Thankfully, we were not asked where we were grazing our flock.

This time walking past the shepherd shop we passed an open fronted butchers and sitting on a chair next to the counter and talking with the apron wearing proprietor was KENNY! This time a photo opportunity was thwarted by a combination of our surprise, the narrowness of the street, the abundance of sharp instruments near at hand to 'Kenny' if he took umbrage at our paparazzi attempts. The photo would have to wait another day but we had a location we could visit on future expeditions to raise our chances of capturing an image. Future trips to the town drew a blank despite sitting watching the world go by in the square and casually walking by the butchers shop. One of the other attractions of the town was a small park with a taverna in one corner serving lovely traditional meals at a good price with cool seating under a canopy where the tables faced the park.

It was after a pleasant lunch one day at this taverna that as we walked across the park back to the car we suddenly spied Kenny right next to us sitting on a bench and as we couldn't stop ourselves staring at him he seemed to make some expression of recognition in a bizarre sort of winking movement involving shutting one eye and by stretching his jaw down opening the other eye wider. We walked on too confused to attempt to explain our quest and totally avoiding any attempts at a photo. "I think we better call this off now - we got in too deep." It was agreed we would try other forms of more harmless entertainment whilst staying on the island - the Kenny quest was over for us. As sometimes happens having lowered our expectations we were surprised to find that some months later on revisiting the town we found Kenny sitting on

the same bench in apparent deep conversation with another bearded but less lookalike 'Kenny'.

The opportunity was too good to miss and this time using the telephoto lens I captured his image for posterity. The quest was completed - we beat a retreat.

Strangely since the photo op and many visits to the same town Kenny has never been seen by us again - maybe he's had a drastic haircut?

In recent times I have gone for a safer pursuit on the island. I am not sure whether it will capture the public as much the 'Men who looked like Kenny Rogers site.' I have yet to test it but I started to notice rocks with faces. Some samples are shown her including spectacular tribute to media superstar and famous fox: Basil Brush and several other finds.

15 Raki

I must have led a sheltered life as I had not heard of or encountered raki, (or in local village speak *Raachi*) until we first came to the island. It's a clear strong spirit manufactured from grape pressings or so I have been told and it appears that licensing regulations are relaxed enough that it's made as a sort of home brew. It is traditional for a small flask and glasses to be brought to your table at the end of a meal sometimes with a complimentary sweet course. I am pleased if it's a plate of fresh fruit as grapes, apple slices or melon pieces dipped in the spirit is my preferred way to consume it. There are other traditions that seem to be associated with it. Men will often throw it down like a shot and then slam the empty glass on the table where it is refilled. We also suffered on evening in one of the family restaurants where, after already relaxing from a hearty meal with plentiful wine we were brought a small flask and drank it slowly whilst listening to the owners son playing traditional music on a lyra. When the performance had finished we clapped Iorgo enthusiastically as it was clear that he had musical skills. He came over to our table with another flask and explained this was from his father, the owner of the restaurant. He pointed at a bearded gentleman closer to our age sitting in the corner and we both raised glass to one another. We drank two small glasses each of the strong spirit emptying the flask but to our alarm Iorgo brought another full flask. We didn't know whether to refuse was bad etiquette so we compromised by ordering a flask for Iorgo and his father and drank just half of our flask before insisting on getting the bill and paying it while I could still see and stand up. In future I vowed to always leave a little in the flask to demonstrate clearly that we had finished for the night.

Other times particularly if it's a lunch time meal on leaving you be handed a small recycled water bottle with the hushed description -"this is my raki - the best!.' I carry a recurrent dread of leaving one of these in the hire car - like a lurking unexploded bomb; either waiting to spontaneously combust or almost as bad being mistaken for a refreshing drink of water - a large swig of which would probably immediately exceed the breathalyser limit. Thankfully, neither of these have yet occurred though I do speculate how debilitating a new arrival at night at the airport would find their first drive on the always exciting Cretan National Road unwittingly enlivened by a hearty swig from a forgotten raki water bottle found in the hire car.

The discovery of the Raki industry cleared up another mystery when we had spotted what looked like Anthony Gormley's foray into recreating the Clangers, (fans of 1970's TV will recognise the likeness.) They looked ancient and apparently they are distillation vessels for creating the raki spirit but I quite like them as some kind of metallic homage to the Clangers.

The abundance of the free raki bottles and the occasional house warming gift of a bottle - again the promise -" this is my own or my uncle's/brother's/father's raki - the best!" meant some kind of plan of action was required. We had heard it recommended for aching joints and muscles but currently not suffering from those problems and also not wanting to go about in the day time smelling of spirits for obvious reasons, the smell in a hot car could be dangerous! A cafe owner in the town recommended soaking fruit in a bottle with a little sugar and turning it daily for a couple of weeks before straining of the fruit. This process seemed similar to making sloe gin so certainly sounded an option and we may end up with a more palatable drink. We experimented with lemon, strawberries and cherries but balked at the suggestion of coffee to produce a Cretan Tia Maria drink. It was a success and proved to be a welcome gift in small bottles to give to friends so the surplus problem was solved.

16 Archeology

For some visitors to Crete the wealth of archaeological site on the island is a major attraction. I had always been impressed by the abundance of the sites but also by their similarity to modern day hill villages. This is not true of the royal palaces like Knossos and Malia both of which we have visited and both we vowed to return at a quieter time to try and avoid the crowds. The sites that I found more interesting were the Minoan towns like Gournia to the south of us set in an idyllic position near the coast and covering a relatively large area of hillside sloping towards the sea. Walking around the site, the width of the streets and the footprints of the small houses and the rooms within were so close in scale and layout to our own and many other traditional villages on the island.

We could imagine our own village would look very similar if all the houses were demolished to leave their walls only one metre high and the remaining walls in this ancient town appeared of very similar construction to what we have seen of our own stone walls during the renovation process.

Archeologists have dated the settlement back to 3000 BC but have since concluded that part of the original town was levelled around 1700 BC for the construction of a small palace.

At its most populous the town was estimated to have population of some 4000 but excavations suggest the palace was destroyed by fire around 1450 BC , a time when every major Minoan centre was destroyed or abandoned.

The town was excavated in the early 20th century and is one of the Minoan settlements to be fully excavated. The town lies on small hill a few hundred metres from the coast and the Gulf of Mirabello. The location is an important one lying on the logical east west route across the island but also near the north south route at the narrowest point of the island. The routes avoid the mountain heights allowing easier communications. The town was thought to extend down towards the seashore and evidence of seashore installations with excavations by archaeologists naming a 'Shore House' thought to be a ship shed used as a long and narrow form of boat house. It was a large building estimated as at least 25 by 10 metres with incorporating storage rooms as well as the ship stalls. There are also the remains of pier type promontory foundations both above water level and extending below the water.

These are fascinating remains and the Gournia site is heartily recommended for a visit but for us the most interesting detail in writings about the site is the reference to Minoan houses.I quote :-
"An idea of what Minoans Houses looked like can be gained from the ivory plaques discovered in the East wing of Knossos. These plaques show what houses in the town of Knossos looked like in the 17th century BC.
On the roof there was a small room. This may have been used for sleeping in during the hot summer months. The rooms on the first floor had windows but those on the ground floor did not, although some of them had doors on the ground floor. It may be that windows on the ground floor were avoided for simple reasons of security. The houses were built around a wooden frame -wooden beams run horizontally and were linked to upright beams, the most likely reason for the use of these beams was as protection against earthquake damage."

I was astounded reading this as the description so closely matched our own house before the renovation. The ground floor lacked a window, these were on the first floor and the construction was reinforced with timbers. As part of the rebuilding works these were replaced with a steel frame construction - as earthquake protection! There was also mention of access between floors by wooden ladders through a trapdoor inside the house . Shown below is the hatch and ladder staircase when we first saw the house.

One thing that had always fascinated me about the island was the abundance of stones. Where in Britain fields would be sub-divided by hedgerows here there were miles and miles of dry stone walls. The stones were often used for elaborate terracing following the steep contours of the mountains but the surprising thing was the fields and landscapes were still covered in large stones. The rural depopulation and abandonment was not enough to explain the quantity. It seemed as if despite all the traditional houses, the original paved tracks and the boundary walls using these stones there was still just too many to allow the clearance of the land. To me it was a mystery.

17 Triandafyllos

One of our favourite restaurants in our early stays was in the
next village where you ate out of doors, under the stars with a
menu that was all mezes and predominantly vegetable dishes.
They were always delicious and reasonably priced and
accompanied by metal flasks of the local house wine nicely
chilled. One of the best things about the place was the waiter
who was always welcoming but with a very dry sense of
humour. When it wasn't busy we would pester him with
questions most of which he would answer with a shrug and an
"I don't know — why do you want to know that." He mostly
reserved factual replies for questions about the food or recipes
and in these areas he was helpful. I recall that he was one of
the first people to tell us the name of the place across the
large bay that we discovered was Thripti but when asked what
it would be like he retorted "Cold I should think, like this wine."
One surprise was when we asked his name and although he
warned us it was unusual we were amazed to be told it was
Triandafyllos, which translates as 'Rose' or literally thirty
petals. We were disappointed one year to find the restaurant
all closed up although the furniture was neatly stacked on the
terrace part of which was covered with a rustic sort of wooden
veranda. On later visit we discovered that it had reopened but
the new proprietor lamented that trade was very slow as
people seemed to have forgotten about it and in truth it was
little way out of the town and up a hill that might deter casual
visits. Anyway, we stayed and had a meal that was as good as
it had always been, fava, several different bean dishes,
courgette balls, grilled aubergines, spicy cheese dips,
meatballs and peppers in oil accompanied by home baked
bread and local wine. When we finished the owner shared a
flask of raki with us and on hearing our house was in the upper
village offered us a lift home which was tempting but we
politely refused saying that the walk up would help us sleep
but we promised to return. The food was so good that we
returned the following week bringing two friends who had a
shop in the resort. They enjoyed the meal but again we were
the only diners. It was in the earlier days of social media and I
suggested that they try to promote the business on Tripadvisor

which I wasn't sure that he saw the point of and our friends also promised to promote the business to customers of their shop in the town.

I thought no more about it but I was pleased to see the following spring that as we walked past one evening the restaurant seemed full; so full that we walked by suggesting we went on to somewhere quieter.

But the owner had other plans calling out to us -"Hey Geoff, come in. I want to thank you so much - after your visit last year your friends kept sending us new customers and we have a good Tripadvisor score and things are going so well. I want to thank you for your help you must eat here - on the house!" We were ushered in and treated like honoured guests. We had to go into the kitchen where his wife was the chef for her to also thank us and a space was cleared out front for a table for us and we ate a lovely meal for free. Maybe 'what goes around comes around' as they say.

18 Wine

Crete has vineyards and produces some very good wines that are rarely seen in Britain. We had seen vineyards on some of the plateaus and had noticed the vines tended to be low growing and wired differently to farming methods noticed in Italy or Spain. Our eating out is frequent enough that we control our budget by sticking to the local wines served in half or one kilo metal jugs and this white wine is usually served chilled and tends to be quite light and refreshing.

When a new taverna opened in our village our first meal there was accompanied by the local wine and as sometimes happens a free drink is provided at the end of the meal. As we paid our bill a large jug of wine was brought to our table. Not wishing to offend we explained we had only arrived that afternoon and had some unpacking and sorting out to do at our house.

"Where is your house?" I pointed out through the side window and said "it's just at the back there - we are neighbours."

"Take the jug home with you - it will help you with your unpacking. You can bring the jug back tomorrow - if we are not open just leave it at the door."

On returning the jug the following day to make conversation I said how much we had enjoyed the meal and the wine. "The wine can be brought in town -you can keep the box in your fridge - cheaper than buying bottles." Always having an eye for a bargain and knowing that the jugs in the taverna were priced at only 3 or 6 euros I enquired where it would find the boxes for sale.

"You know Andreas at the bottom of the hill going into town?" 'Isn't that the butchers?" I asked curiously. "Yes, he is my friend -tell him Ianni sent you. He will give you my price if you are lucky." So later that week I was found parking nearby and entering the first butchers shop I had tried to buy drinks in.

'Hello, we have had your wine at Ianni's taverna - he said I could buy it here'

"Of course, white or red my friend"

'White please.' "The same as Ianni has - twenty five litres, is your car nearby - it's quite heavy!" I roughly calculated this would be over 5 gallons and would weigh around 50 pounds but also be likely to completely fill the fridge and outlast our three week stay by some margin.

'Um. that's probably more than I want - is it the only size you have?"

"Oh no - 20 litres. or 15"

'Any smaller?' I asked tentatively.

"10 litres" - then almost dismissively "we also have the smaller 5 litres"

I think that would probably suit us to start with and one was produced from behind the counter.

"Nine euros" - 'pardon nine?' - "Of course."

I thanked him, paid and staggered out of the butchers with the smallest wine box he had for sale and the largest one I had ever bought whilst wondering how much the price per litre fell if bought in bulk, say twenty-five litres bulk. Also working out the profit margin in tavernas on their wine jug sales. Still, I repeat, I love a bargain.

19 Musings

No, nothing to do with museums. Just thoughts on how life continuously changes and however you plan and prepare for events life is unlikely to be the way you anticipate. I have mentioned before that the kitchen requirements turned out to be less extensive than we might have originally thought; this was for a number of reasons. One was the abundance of great and inexpensive places to eat and because of this it was more common to meet socially in a restaurant or bar and share the bill. Another reason was the climate and great supply of fresh local ingredients meant a cold spread with salad ingredients and cold meats and cheeses was often preferable to a hot meal. Also the long hours that the shops in town were open meant daily shopping for fresh food could be undertaken in the evening as well as the day, so it was unnecessary to do 'big shops' or stockpile. Sadly, in recent years the reduction in the village of the elderly 'yia-yias' and the likelihood that most villagers now owned a car meant that the vans calling to the village whilst not stopping entirely had certainly become less frequent with their visits.

We realised that we had been coming to the area now for long enough to observe and experience social changes. Certainly the village itself was quieter generally than in the early years with the closing recently of the last kafenion and although a taverna had opened it was more likely to be open in the evening and out of the main tourist season, only at the weekends. Friends in the village recently gave us the good news that one of the closed kafenions was being renovated by a new owner and we hope when it reopens it will bring a little more life back into the village. Certainly it will be welcomed both by villagers but also by people who have made the effort to walk up to the village from the coast and would welcome some refreshment.

Other noticeable changes - even possible to see from our roof terrace is the development of pockets of cultivation on ground around the village previously neglected. This is surely a by-product of what is called the 'Crisis' post the 2009 banking

76

crash and the extreme difficulties experienced by the Greek economy in particular. The small-holding areas are very productive with several growing seasons in one year, providing a number of consecutive crops of beautiful fruits and vegetables. This is also supplemented by small scale livestock rearing with chickens and small flocks of sheep and goats. It may have been born out of financial necessity but there is also some pride shown in the neat cultivation of the areas and attending to livestock, usually in the cooler evenings and probably after a day's work at the day job or before an evening's shift in a restaurant.

Another trend seems to be a growing enthusiasm to renovate the old small village houses. When our own restoration project was taking place a small number of others in our village, and I'm aware this was repeated in other villages around about, were being restored by foreign owners, usually for use as holiday homes. In recent times similar houses have been restored by Cretan families, sometimes for letting, but often for use as a permanent home for younger Cretans as their homes. Conversations with young locals confirm that these houses are being seen as desirable and their position in a village away from the busier towns and resort areas providing a welcome respite after a busy day at work. A conversation with a friend in the village who was a few years younger than us fleshed out the details of how life had been in the village within living memory. We were aware that before the large hotels had been built in the late 1960 and 70's the seafront around the harbour had been smaller and less developed than the adjacent surrounding villages. He recalled some dozen kafenions and a score of shops. The school was in the village next to the church in the building that still exists today and around 700 people lived in the village. The shops covered the whole range of foodstuffs with two butchers but also included one mens tailor and two dressmakers, a hairdresser/barber, a shoemaker and two saddlers as well as hardware and metalworkers. There were bakeries where as well as providing bread and pastries for sale the large ovens were used by villagers to bring and cook their own dishes of briam, moussaka and stifado etc. The village had a meat safe and ice man came from the next town to deliver ice that was brought by boat. He also mentioned that the day was structured differently with sleep from 7 pm and awakening at midnight to feed the animals so that they had energy when the working day started at dawn to avoid the heat of the day. The men with go to the kafenion for refreshment after the feeding and before the working day.

I recalled how busy the village had been in the first year we had moved into the house when a Greek tv series was being filmed using the old houses and the narrow alleys to simulate Spinalonga, the leper colony for the story of 'The Island.' (I recounted our brief career as TV stars acting as lepers in a hospital scene for two days in my earlier book.) As it was the tourist season the actual leper colony could not be used so a film set was recreated in the village and for control over lighting much of the shooting of scenes took place under artificial lighting, often until 3 o'clock in the morning. With drinks and coffees between takes from the two kafenions that remained open it must have seemed like old times to some of the villagers.

The village began to change with the building of the first hotels through the 1970's and new apartment blocks on the coast and from that time the village declined and houses were abandoned. He said that from this time work opened up in tourism as well as building trades and replaced agriculture and the whetstone and salt production that were the previous local industries.

Other changes we noticed almost ran in opposing directions. There was the spread of globalisation and the changes that unchecked could make everywhere in the world seem the same. Whilst the town was some way off opening a Starbucks or a McDonalds the sense of adventure on shopping expedition had started to evaporate when stocks of Colgate, Nescafe and recognisable brands from home appeared alongside the local products. It always contained a spirit of mystery buying a bottle of 'Fabuloso' or 'Mr Proper' and not being sure whether to wash the floor or your hair with it. Judging by the picture -maybe not the hair.

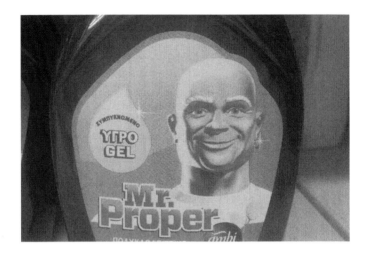

In a counter direction we sensed a new pride in things local. The clothes boutiques and galleries on the island were at great pains to emphasis 'made in Crete or Greece' as mark of quality. This trend was becoming noticeable in the tavernas and restaurants where these in the tourist areas had previously served cuisine closer to international recipes, steaks, burgers etc and a need to track down establishments serving the traditional vegetable orientated dishes where these were seen as an integral part rather than a 'side dish.'

Now 'horta' seasonal boiled greens, a cretan superfood was not so hard to track down, and Briam and Kleftiko dishes were readily available and signs outside restaurants boasted 'traditional local dishes.'

20 Ianni's Improvements

We knew that owning an old house particularly one that is not
inhabited for part of the year would entail maintenance
commitments and this has turned out to be the case with the
small house. I have written about the problems with uninvited
guests of the non-human variety but there were also the
refinements mentioned earlier to the services. This had
introduced us to Ianni the builder and his expertise. Our next
requirement was related to water but this time not the piped
variety. In spring when we returned after the house was
unoccupied through the winter we had started to notice some
dried water mark runs on the mortar between the stones on
two of the walls in the upstairs room. We had experienced
some rains there but know that the winter rains could be
torrential so were not surprised to see what I understood to be
'water ingress' in the stone walls which were the ones facing
the coast and the prevailing weather. Ianni was called and we
arranged with him to come to the house - I made the request
in slow English which I knew he had a better understanding of
than my non-existent Albanian. I then repeated the
arrangements using rudimentary Greek which relied on my
knowledge of the words for house, work, water and tomorrow -
followed by the one English word we often exchanged in
connection with the house - 'Problem.'
From what I could gather he would arrive the next day in the
morning and it would be 'no problem!'
Good as his word, or what I thought we had agreed, Ianni
came to the house before 9 a.m. the next morning and came
upstairs where I pointed out the dried out water trails on the
mortar, coming halfway down the walls between the stones of
the walls. 'Ah' and to my barely disguised joy Ianni said
'Problem!' accompanied by one of his grins. 'Pano' - indicating
the roof terrace as he led the way up the spiral stairs to the
terrace. It was already warming up there as he leaned over the
stone parapet and patted the wall facing the sea then,
alarmingly he leapt up onto the tiled roof and crouching at the
edge leaning over to further inspect the wall. Coming back
onto the roof terrace floor he patted the top of the parapet wall
and pointed at some hairline cracks between the mortar -

"Problem" - so the source of the leakage had been discovered. Ianni then indicated with the flat of his hands a smoothing over the walls. The visit was concluded by an arrangement to meet and talk in town that evening in the kafenion with the added comment of 'Elvis.' It was clear that for the final arrangement of the details Ianni's teenage son was being drafted in again to reprise his role as English -Albanian interpreter as neither of us had yet to master one another's native languages well enough to solve the 'Problem.'

We hadn't made any plans for supper in town as the last meeting and conversation at the kafenion with Ianni and Elvis had culminated with a large chip omelette. Hands were shaken, cheeks were kissed and beers ordered. Elvis arrived wearing a T shirt of one of the steak houses in the main square, 'I deliver for them in the evening,' - we started asking him all the embarrassing questions parents and their contemporaries ask the young, 'Have you finished your studies? Are you planning to join your father in the family business?

A knowing look was exchanged between father and son and a few words spoken by Ianni clearly for Elvis to translate - "My father says my sister is studying to be a nurse …..' We recognised a strong hint so I thought it prudent to change the subject. "Can you ask your father what he thinks needs to be done to our house, when it can be done and an idea of the price." From experience we felt we knew the answer to the last question - it was likely to be 500 euros. There was a discussion in Albanian and some meaningful silences and looking at his phone screen by Ianni which we presumed contained diary details of his work commitments. Eventually, Elvis translated that a thick waterproof rendering coat would be applied to the two walls at terrace level with a coating to cover the top of the terrace parapet walls at least that's what I thought but I must have looked a little perplexed as Ianni pulled a pen from his shirt and drew a small sketch on paper napkin to clearly show where the coating would be applied and as an afterthought wrote 500 € below the sketch. I wisely resisted shouting 'Yes' and punching the air. Elvis announced that he needed to go to work but promised that if we needed a delivery of pitta gyros or pizza it would come very quickly. Given that he was definitely the only delivery driver on the island that knew

where our house without an address was we readily agreed we would be taking up his offer at some stage. 'My Dad says he can do the work next week - he will text you.'
I looked forward to my first text message in Albanian.
The work was completed in the early part of the following week and as part of the work involved carrying buckets of mixture through the house we wisely left Ianni with a spare key and made ourselves scarce for some of the day. When it was finished it looked good and actually improved the profile of the house but perhaps more importantly successfully sealed the walls against 'winter storm leakage.'

The next house job that we asked Ianni to carry out was improving the stairs. The original stairs were a metal framework topped with some kind of marble slabs as the treads and backs. The stairs turned through ninety degrees after a square step part of the way up. The top flight had opaque glass uprights to the treads to let more light into the wet room below. We had been involved in much of the material selection during the protracted renovation of the house and we were happy with most of the selections, the grey stone slabs for the window sills, the wood lintels and reused ceiling beams upstairs but we couldn't recall choosing the stone on the stairs. Furthermore the treads didn't go right across the stairwell with small metal troughs at the side described as a benefit by the architect and he suggested they could be used to form 'memory pockets' into which we could put shells and stones and other found treasures. To us they always seemed dust-traps. I had suspected that the stone had come from an excess on another job rather than been specified for our house but this was only a suspicion. The stone matched in colour with the floor tiles downstairs but the steps had sharp edges and we had concluded wood would be preferable and there was a further advantage that we could arrange access to storage below rather than through the back of the wet room where I had installed two small doors, The space below had plumbing and power arranged for a washing machine and installation of this would be easier if a hatch was put in. Time to call Ianni. The usual cryptic conversation took place along with an attempt at describing in greek 'changing the stairs from stone to wood. That was what I thought I said at any rate. Later that week at a pre-arranged morning Ianni appeared with a new worker, his carpenter presumably as he was described as 'working in wood.' The conversation mainly took place through the medium of mime and all seemed to go reasonably smoothly apart from a rather congested session of mime in the tiny wet room below the stairs which was reminiscent of Dad's Army in the episode where the entire platoon follow Captain Mannering into his office and crush him behind his desk. This was re-enacted with the three of us, S. wisely not joining in that part of the discussion. It was agreed that we didn't want to lose the glass backs on the top half of the staircase so the work would just cover half the stairs but the gaining of easier storage space with a hinged hatch was a real bonus as storage space was at premium in the house. For a change there was not mention of the normal 500 € as the wood would need pricing.

We stayed out of the way for a couple of mornings and thankfully at the end of the first day the old stone treads and been removed and some wood treads were in place so it looked like we could sleep upstairs. The second day saw finishing work and a hinged hatch to our understairs storage installed. Much to my joy the bill was less than the standard 500 euros and as a bonus we were asked if some of the offcuts were if use to us. As we had storage in the apothiki it would be a pity to refuse the offer so I know I had some wood to use somewhere when I had the inspiration and enthusiasm. So another improvement with the help of Ianni. Given previous incident in the cupboard I couldn't help thinking of the work as the 'Rat trapdoor.'

21 Floats

We had always enjoyed exploring the small mountain roads towards the north coast above the village. There were a few kafenions and tavernas in the scattered villages as well as spectacular scenery particularly as you dropped down to the coast which was much more rugged than near us and much of the coastline in the south of the island. With large breakers and rough seas it was easy to recognise the predicament of someone who told us a story when we were queuing in the tax office. She was a Canadian lady who was rather distraught and had been told in the mobile phone shop that they were unable to sell her a handset and a sim for a mobile phone without a greek tax number and a greek address. They had been sailing around the islands and in a storm north of Crete their boat had almost capsized and in the drama had lost some bags and possessions overboard including their mobile phones. What could they do? I thought we would be likely to be called up to the counter ahead of her as we had already been there when she arrived and had noticed her as she looked distressed. We told her not to worry as someone would advise her -"But I don't speak greek - will you interpret." I explained that my greek would probably not stretch to such an explanation and briefly rehearsed in my head the mime for a ship in a storm and items going overboard but looking at the ages of the office staff I was sure there would be the chance to discuss the problem in English. I was called to the counter while S. sat with her and I asked before dealing with our tax payment whether someone could help the lady with her phone problem in English. The reply was one that was very familiar through experience - "Of course, bring her over," much to her relief and expressing her gratitude to us she was handed some forms and whilst we were paying our bill at the next counter some of the forms were stamped and she was advised to return to the phone shop where "All would be OK." It was one of the many examples of things working out.

The advantage of the rough conditions on this coast was that it was a good beach combing location and whilst we weren't looking for washed up treasure there was some interesting driftwood, sea urchins, shells and a certain amount of cork fishing net floats and it was these that caught our eye. it wasn't long before these became a reason to visit these desolate and deserted stretches of rocky beaches. The chance of a cold drink or even a fish lunch in one of the out of the way tavernas where you good be sure of a good value meal as well as warm welcome. We had taken to calling one of the fish restaurants 'The Restaurant at the End of the Universe' referencing the Hitchhikers Guide to the Galaxy. it was christened because I nearly drove the car into the sea as the road ended in a dead end somewhat abruptly with a drop to the beach and little space to turn around. The 'other world' character of the area was confirmed when we spotted a garden filled with random objects as a sort of outsider art installation or at least that's what it looked like to us.

Another intriguing find at the north coast was a building wedged below a rock outcrop. It is pictured below and we assumed it was a small chapel of possibly a refuge for retreats. We had encountered one of these on the south coast near a monastery but separate from it. That one was supplied with blankets, matches and candlesticks, bottled water and beer and some monastery bread. We had seen these through an open door. The north coast building was rather less hospitable with a locked door. Nevertheless, it was still an interesting piece of architecture.

The float collection became one of the personal decorative touches back at the house where a line of several dozen all repainted in different colours trailed across a ledge half way up the stairs where the upstairs wall was set back as a different thickness to the downstairs.

22 Monasteries & Churches

To the north of us were a number of monasteries, one the Areti monastery had a beautiful courtyard garden with a small church, two chapels and fruit trees, pools and caged birds. It was always a restful and cooler place to visit on a warm day as it sat on the side of the hill and the garden had cooling winds blowing through it. It dates back to the late 16th century and is one of the fortified monasteries on the islands and is surrounded outside the high stone walls by twelve ancient cypress trees said to represent the twelve apostles.

Nearby is another smaller monastery, Karamoutsas with a beautiful vaulted hall that on one visit we found a number of the ladies in the village clearing away dishes and platters from what looked a jolly good feast the night before. It was good to think these buildings still were used because it was rare for us to see a monk or even any sign of habitation yet the grounds were well tended in both and the churches immaculately kept often with candles burning inside.

Visitors could add to the candles by leaving a few coins as an offering and lighting one of the long thin candles and placing them alongside others in a bed of sand in a tray near the church entrance. Sometimes there were hunks of cinnamon 'holy bread' in a basket and maximum kudos was gained on returning to the village if one or more of the yia yias were to be found sitting in the street outside their house to hand the bread over to. The message 'from Karidi' would be met with a flurry of chest crossing as well as an expression of thanks usually reinforced with clasping of hands.

I recall a visit to another monastery which we had seen a sign post to from a junction on the road to the south coast and had been told there was view point where it was possible to see both coastlines of the north and south coasts at the same time. (Presumably a turning of the head through 180 degrees would also be required but this hadn't been specified.) We thought our trip out could combine the two destinations and on the map it looked near to the village of Episkopi the village with the 10th century church and as significantly, the home of the one euro lunch mentioned earlier. The drive up to the monastery certainly started to give spectacular views although the higher we climbed the view seemed to get hazier and the air felt less dry with more vegetation at the roadside instead of bleached out grasses and olive trees. I have since looked up the history of the Faneromeni monastery and it apparently dates back to the 1450's AD and looking at my photos I can see old buildings set into the cliffside but my recollection was of a modernist building with large expanses of whitewashed terraces set to take advantage of the views. There is also a modern cloister painted in similar colour ways to the restored Knossos palace with ochre and pale colour washes. Walking under an arch into a courtyard we found we were almost alone. I say almost as a small cat followed us in and one monk was sitting on a stone bench scrutinising the screen of a mobile phone. Along the wall from him chained to a bird table on a stand was a large blue and yellow macaw parrot. The table was covered with a newspaper and a sprinkling of bird seed. The parrot appeared to be reading the newspaper and it briefly paused the study of this to look at us momentarily before silently going back to the newspaper. It may have been counting it's bird seed but it was pretty intent on continuing what it was doing and definitely not being distracted from this by us. Similarly, the monk only paused from his phone for a few seconds to nod and smile to us before his concentration reverted to the phone screen. The cat had disappeared to be replaced by a young golden labrador who briefly greeted us in silence before wandering off through an open doorway. The whole place was eerily quiet and I would not have been wholly surprised at any other creatures suddenly materialising and going away again. We cautiously took a few photos of the monastery and the view, left some coins in the collection plate by the gate and nodding our goodbyes to the monk and the

parrot left through the archway. Back at the car we agreed it seemed strange. We were aware some monasteries operated under vows of silence but extending this to their resident livestock was an escalation of this and a little unnerving. Still it made for a peaceful afternoon outing!
We didn't see the trans island vista but found this at a later date miles away on a different road - I had been given false information second or third hand -maybe I should have asked the monk - or the parrot?

Even our village was blessed with three churches as well as graveyard in the edge of the village where small glass shrines often had candles lit inside them at night requiring a relative or church elder to attend each evening to light or replenish. Similar small shrines with miniature buildings inside glass cases regularly occurred at the roadside. These were often sited at the roadside on sharp bends often with steep drops from the road. I had speculated they were placed as memorials for fatal accidents on the roads but had yet to find the right opportunity to sensitively have this confirmed.

Of the village churches the largest is named St George and is regularly used for services with the bell being rung to remind the congregation.
I have only peeped inside through an open door and very fine it looked too but the other family member had a more memorable experience. One Saturday S. announced she would get up early the following day and attend the morning church service. Leaving me in bed with a welcome cup of coffee she followed the sound of the summoning church bell up to the main village church less than five minutes walk from our house. All went well she later told me and was flattered to be called over by several of the village ladies, dressed in their finest who shuffled to make a space on the bench seat to accommodate her. The service was an experience and culminated by the small congregation standing at the end and moving towards the altar, apparently to be greeted by the priest. S. was propelled along by her posse of village Yia Yias until she realised that this was to take communion which consisted of a healthy slug of red wine and chunk of flavoured bread, (none of your watered down C of E wine and tiny wafers!) The event was memorable but made a little more alarming back in Sussex when a casual enquiry of the Greek Orthodox priest at our Greek classes brought the following stern warnings. Communion only be given to people confirmed in the Greek church and only when they have attended a confessional in the previous month. She wisely kept her own counsel on the misdemeanour not wishing to risk expulsion or worse from Greek school.

The other two churches in the village are much smaller and we have only seen them closed. Down in town is a larger church that is used more regularly and we have witnessed weddings, funerals and processions on name and saints days.

23 Deserted Villages

I had never entirely understood the number of empty derelict houses on the island and not just individual houses but some whole villages. Was it part of an exodus to the larger towns and the coast from the countryside or were the tourism developments wholly to blame moving the employment from agriculture to services? Perhaps the old houses were considered unsuitable for modern life with people preferring modern apartments as part of an urbanisation movement? In the early 20th century there were also religious expulsions with these balanced by an influx of religious refugees.
We had also been told that inheritance laws complicated property ownership and with family members have moved away often abroad the splitting of ownership made the taking over of old properties through inheritance somewhat complex. We had experienced this with our own house purchase with three family signatures required for the empty property with ownership split through inheritance and just to further complicate matters one of the signatories was in hospital and apparently signed it from their hospital bed.
Whatever the causes the countryside was full of empty properties some more easily habitable than others. Even in our own village with beautiful scenic views and proximity to a popular resort on the coast there were at least a dozen empty properties that we passed on our three minute walk from the car park to our house. In the whole village there were at least as many again.
Studies suggest that the rural population on the island was at a peak circa 1950, totalling some 350,000 and in recent times had fallen to only half of that figure, (of a total modern island population of over 500,000.)
Derelict villages have an eerie air all of their own. Often houses through broken windows or open doors revealed furnishings still in place even though other evidence suggested abandonment many years earlier. We found these places fascinating although our enthusiasm was tempered by the sight of a gang of rats emerging from one house which certainly discouraged us from doing no more in future than peering through doorways or widows.

We found one particularly spectacular abandoned dwelling a short drive up the mountain above us on the crest of the ridge overlooking the village. As on many of these heights there were a number of derelict stone windmills. The position was spectacular looking over our village several hundred metres below and right down to the coast, the bay and the distant mountains. The view from our own roof terrace was spectacular but this was at another level. Already in the lee of the crest some expensive and grand villas had been constructed.

Driving up the track we noticed that the last windmill in a row of three had an extension on it, a single storey building with window openings without window frames, it had the appearance of an abandoned renovation project. Curiosity got the better of us so we walked around the front facing onto a garden area that was overgrown with more evidence of an abandoned building project. There was a doorway but no door so tentatively we went inside after first calling hello, partly in case someone was still actively working on the 'project' but more realistically to scare out any rats, feral cats, bats or any other creatures whose sudden exit could give us a shock. All was quiet, apart from a scrunching underfoot on pieces of gravel and broken plaster, it looked long abandoned although the roof was intact and the floor dry although at this time of the year there hadn't been any recent rainfall. The only light came through the door and window openings. This was different to our own house when we first viewed it when sunlight streamed in through holes between the roof tiles. It was dry and some dividing walls had been re-plastered and in one room the beginnings of a kitchen had been started. What was the story? Why had the renovation stalled? There was no 'VENDEE' sign outside showing it was up for sale. We walked across the terrace carefully avoiding small piles of rubble and patches of thorny weeds and found a small concrete sunken plunge pool at the boundary complete with peeling blue paint often used on pools. What a wonderful position to float in on a hot day admiring the view.

Of course that evening, on our roof terrace with glasses of wine looking up at the mountain behind - "I think I can just see the top of the windmill."

"The view was spectacular - you could do something with that garden- wouldn't the round rooms in the windmill be interesting rooms to design - and a viewing gallery at the top! The roof seemed intact - there must be services laid to the road. We know Ianni now - he's very reliable. Wasn't there a kafenion in the nearby village? There was taverna but it seems closed now. That evening we walked into town through the olive groves, a matter of under twenty minutes downhill. A little longer to walk back up or a five euro taxi ride and five minutes.

"The road up there is horrendous, deep ravine one side- very narrow if a coach or lorry comes- you wouldn't want to walk up to it - certainly not in the dark.
We don't know who owns it - maybe the building permit was not granted. What if the was an earthquake up there on the mountain. We've just got our house finished - its much more lock up and leave, low utility bills and taxes and we don't really use it enough - we'd have to come and supervise the building - we'd have to sell ours to buy it and rent while the work went on. It would be bigger - people would want to come and stay - we'd be running a hotel!" We had heard this as a common complaint from owners with larger houses who had become informal unpaid hoteliers.

By the time we reached town for our supper we had reached a mutual conclusion - let someone else renovate it - it will be definitely more difficult than they first imagine.

On the subject of hotels someone we vaguely knew who keenly photographed derelict buildings had once shown us photos of an abandoned resort hotel on the south coast of the island and I remembered this one day over a lunch in Ierapetra on the south coast.
'He said it was to the west just out of town - let's drive that way and see if we can see it.' By some fluke we found it. Parking the car at the gate we walked down the drive towards the main building past a series of elaborate empty blue swimming pools surrounded by fixed beach style bamboo umbrellas made of thick bamboo canes. painted white with the paint flaking off. Weeds grew through the paving and the whole place was eerily still, there were still curtains at some of the windows.

It was difficult to imagine it with hundreds of guests and the hustle and bustle that would bring.It felt that we were intruding on a past tragedy - at the same time we agreed we were uncomfortable - it seemed to symbolise the fragile veneer of civilisation, almost as if the island which in many ways had so readily embraced modern international tourism was in some areas rejecting it. A more plausible explanation was given later in town by a friend explaining that some hoteliers are so financially stretched that the failure to secure a contract with a travel company can lead to closure and they may not reopen. We had seen some unfinished shells of hotels at a number of places on the island and each time we passed we speculated whether they would ever be completed. Checking this hotel today the website still exists but it suggests the hotel closed early in the 21st century - a ghost website complete with a booking form . I am tempted to fill it in to see if I get a response.

24 Bills

Along with the creative and enjoyable aspects of acquiring a new home such as decorating and furnishing there are also the more mundane matters that require attention such as utility bills and property taxes. We were trying to keep things reasonably simple by limiting services to water and electricity and avoiding such frivolous luxuries as a phone line and internet connection. We didn't have a TV although the greek system cunningly assumes everyone has a TV and puts the charge for the licence on the electricity bill. Whether it is possible to have it removed we have never found out and it is considerably less than the UK though I am unable to confirm whether it is better value. Certainly, it doesn't annoy me so much as I don't watch greek TV; a policy I have begun to adopt in the UK in respect of most news programmes which to me seem mainly speculation about what might happen rather than what I previously understood the news to be a service telling me what had happened.

Thing have changed in the time we have owned the house with mobile contracts giving a good service and unlimited data allowing iPads to substitute for tv in the house. But in earlier times the first electricity bill was something of a mystery. To begin with there was no address for the house, only the PO box in town where it was delivered. Among all the reference numbers on the bill we were able to find a number which matched the number on the electricity meter outside the house so the charges did at least relate to our house. Our meter box was an anonymous beige which happily matched the colour wash on our walls so I didn't have to go to the trouble of painting it to match the walls or shutters which seemed to be the practice here. A particularly artistic example is pictured here for ebook readers. Print book readers can imagine the shades of green or refer to the book illustrations at Pinterest -see https://www.pinterest.es/geoffdendle/life-in-a-small-house-in-crete/

Back to the bill - we enlisted the help of a local friend, Ken who seemed well versed in local matters having run businesses on the island with his wife Barbara and built their own beautiful house there with amazing panoramic views of the whole lagoon. "I see you have come off the builders supply - you have a domestic tariff"

'That's good?' I asked.

"Yes of course, cheaper but more importantly it means your house is legal and has been signed off by the authorities with no outstanding taxes to be paid"

This was welcome good news as visits to the tax office whilst reasonably sociable and the staff helpful were often time consuming and not a little confusing and in our experience - best avoided. The explanation of the rest of the bill was reasonably straight forward including the extra euros charge for our TV licence for our non existent TV and the amount to pay was not going to break the bank. I asked if we could set up a direct debit but was advised that this would be possible only from a greek bank account which we had but had not really actively used it since the completion of the house and the branch we used was in the next town.

We planned a visit to the electricity office where we could ask about direct debits and at the same time pay the bill. Feeling we were making progress and feeling mightily reassured about the legality of the house having heard some horror stories ✗ about ownership and boundary disputes, I brought up the subject of our water bill. This seemed a simpler document the water company not being as cunning as the electricity company in collecting money for services they didn't provide. Maybe they should put road tax for cars on there or dog licences a good little earner from people who have neither of these.

'You are in luck the water company offices are in the same street as the electricity one, it's just over the road. "

The experience of paying our bills was a sort of time travel experience. In the 1970's after university I had worked in an electricity board office which pre computerisation seemed a maze of paper. The first visit was to the electricity company office where inside the door was a counter with an efficient lady who was initially happy to take our payment but as I asked her about future payments by direct debit she hesitated. She then called through the door behind her and indicated we should move way from the counter and wait. After a few minutes another smiling lady appeared who looked like her twin sister and indicated we should follow her into the office. The office had another dozen people in the room mostly shouting to each other or into phones. There were piles of paper on the floor and on desks all of which also contained computer terminals some underneath papers. We were offered seats in front of one of the desks and thankfully we were asked in English how she could help us. I explained we had come in to pay our bill but as we did not spend all our time here wanted to establish an automated bank payment, a direct debit or standing order - was this possible.

She scrutinised our bill - "It is a low bill and I can see your house is small -(some charges were calculated in relation to the square meterage of the house so ours showed 40 squares metres.) Is this the real size of it?" It wasn't the first time we had been asked this question but my answer is always the same.

'Yes, really - you can come and measure it." This time it was met with a 'knowing look' which seemed to suggest that such measure would be met with popular rebellion although it would also result in higher receipts for public finances. I explained that we wanted to ensure payment perhaps by some automated means so we could avoid being disconnected. She laughed and waved her hands at the piles of paper around her desk and seemed to suggest we were well down and list for that to happen.

"Let me take your details." which she did by copying them onto a paper form and calling over one of her less shouty colleagues who appeared to be keying them in to the pc. I then offered cash payment for the bill which she readily accepted, giving me change and then vigorously stamping the document several times with an old fashioned rubber stamp.

"You will be sent documents to arrange the direct debit but you can only use a greek bank account." Then lowering her voice she said "I don't trust the banks better to pay cash before placing our three 10 euro notes her desk drawer and giving me the stamped bill and a few coins change.

"If you don't get the form don't worry and come in next time and pay - you won't be disconnected for these small amounts"
I resisted asking her how their billing system found our house as the bill address was only a PO box and our house as I have mentioned before has no number in a 'street with no name' like the U2 song. I think I realised this may demonstrate a level of knowledge that could get me into trouble but I couldn't resist telling her I had once worked for an electricity company.
"Was it like this ?" she asked -' well, a bit I said' although I was aware things in the UK had modernised since the 1970's.
'No - I am retired now -I wouldn't be much help' I replied as I tried to discreetly glance at the piles of paperwork. 'Well, we'll wait for the form in the post.'
We are yet to receive them and now our accountant deals with the bills but she was right - we haven't been disconnected - yet!
We debated whether we had the strength and enthusiasm to pay the water company bill or to go for a mid-morning coffee. We decided we were in the area so clutching our water bill, (for 9 euros) we crossed the road to their offices where inside the

door was a similar glass counter with a similar cashier apparently having a heated argument over a pile of papers with a lady in front of us. We were used to the fact that normal conversations in greek are often conducted more at higher decibels than the more reserved British would employ in public. In our early visits I had often expected what appeared to be heated arguments between men about to result in fisticuffs only for them to conclude with a smile and a pat on the back then walk away to turn and shout what sounded like a final insult from the other side of the road. To me, as a dog owner, it was reminiscent of when you dragged your dog away from another dog they were snapping at for them to issue a last barked challenge from safe distance the other side of the road. Some ten minutes later after a protracted bout of vigorous stamping by the cashier that appeared to be a demonstration that it might be unwise for anyone to consider fisticuffs with her -it was our turn. Before I could say anything she spoke to us in perfect English with negated my normal opening question of 'May we speak in English.'

"She was paying the bills of her whole village - some of them very overdue."

'We have come to pay our first water bill - the current one,' I hastily added.

"That's fine" she said and a ten euro note was handed over, the bill stamped and half of it given back with the one euro coin change and a smile and it all seemed to be going so well that I thought I would broach the subject of direct debits.

Immediately her friendly expression changed -"I hear that they are thinking about it." She said through pursed lips - "If they do then they won't need me!"

We thanked her and left - it was definitely not the time to tell her that I had been responsible for introducing direct debits for electricity payments to three million customers in the south of England, a skeleton best left in the closet in England. Time for a morning coffee instead.

25 Minoans

There is no doubt that the island of Crete has a fascinating history and like many islands there have been series of occupations by different cultures over time. I am certainly not qualified to give a detailed historical explanation of this but as a visitor to the island I have enjoyed the opportunity to learn a little more about this history and in some cases see the

evidence of this.
The island has many archaeological sites, some are popular and will be crowded, at others you may be able to have the place all to yourself. The scale of the palace at Knossos is impressive and although many doubts have been expressed about the accuracy of the restoration and interpretation by Sir Arthur Evans, it is the most popular and best known of the Minoan sites. I would recommend visiting outside the height of the tourist season and avoiding the hottest part of the day. Other sites we have visited including Lato, Gournia, Malia Palace and Phaestos have proved as interesting. The new archeological museum in the capital Heraklion contains a wealth of treasures from the Minoans and provides evidence of

their art and culture that has fascinated many. The island is home to many myths and legends, some having some potential foundation in fact and others quite possibly fanciful.

One of my own experiences was linked to the legend of Atlantis, the legendary advanced civilisation that disappeared below the waves some time in the past. Locals in the resort told of a sunken village in the bay outside the lagoon and confidently stated the clear waters allowed sight of walls and stone structures on the sea bed. Whilst travelling in the mountains we had avoided the opportunity of visiting the birthplace of Zeus the greek god because, well he was fictional, but there were many stories about Atlantis and other sunken cities and it was local and I had a snorkel and mask.

A warm afternoon found me swimming face down away from the shore in relatively shallow clear water. Whilst I am a reasonably confident swimmer having been forced to learn in the cold baths of a boys grammar school which I am grateful for now but wasn't so sure at the time, I am not an experienced 'snorkler', if that is the correct noun. The view of the marine life was interesting and the water certainly more comfortable than the school pool. I was experiencing a sort of altered senses as the sea bed sloped away and I had a feeling of being 'higher up.' Just as the experience of underwater inverted vertigo was intensifying I definitely spotted a network of straight lines of stones on the seabed some way below me. I am ashamed to say that the vertigo sensation had become so strong that I quickly surfaced and turned and swam to the shore. Coming out of the water and exclaiming in what I hoped was my normal voice -"Yes, I've definitely seen something down there that looked like old walls." That ended my personal quest to discover Atlantis. I have since heard that local boats operate a service out into the bay to view 'Atlantis' and this can be had for a modest price, without vertigo!

Recently there has been more research dedicated to the Atlantis myth and some of this has begun to support Crete and the Minoan civilisation as strong candidates for real life origins behind the myth. Research has linked the abandonment of destroyed palaces to traces of volcanic ash at an eruption on Thera and the creation of the distinctive caldera on that island now known as Santorini and theories have been developed over possible a tsunami disaster befalling the Minoans some 3500 years ago. Historical research writings suggest that this sunken city of Olous was once one of the largest population centres for the Minoans and had an estimated population of some 40,000 people which seems amazing. This is a much larger population than currently, even with the tourist hotels. It is said to have been part of a group of cities in that part of the island along with *Latos, Gourtis,* Ierapitna and *Driros* and was in part governed by the city of Knossos this information stemming from stone tablets discovered at Knossos. It was important during the Minoan period from 3000 to 900 BC. It is suggested it was a thriving community with an elected city mayor and its own coinage and water system. The traditional greek gods were worshipped along with their own city goddess, Vritomartis. There are suggestions that the loss of Olous to the sea was most likely as a result of the natural sinking of the east of the island rather than the Thera eruption and this sinking process apparently continues today. There is evidence that the city still existed in some form up until the 2nd century BC. Some archeological relics can be found today in the Archeological museum in Agios Nikolaos.Much of the underwater ruins have gone with the area archaeologically protected to preserve what remains. It is thought much of the building materials were removed during the 15th century Venetian occupation with the stones used to construct the salt pans and the fortress on the island of Spinalonga. Such history continues to reinforce the mythology of the island. Below is a mosaic over the causeway.

26 Wildlife

Apart from the encounters with wildlife inside the house any contact with livestock away from home has been limited.
The village seemed to be populated with flocks of small sparrows and it was good to hear their song and see them flitting between the rooftops. This was a time when gloom mongers at home were predicting great reductions in the native sparrow population. My ornithology knowledge is limited but is it possible they have migrated to a warmer place ?
Trips into the mountains would encounter large herds of goats and sheep, sometimes alerting their presence through the tinkling of their bells before you actually sighted them. This could be helpful on the narrow mountain roads as the road could sometimes be blocked by herds or you could be startled be an agile goat vaulting into the road and off out of it down the slope below. It was rare to see the large vulture birds near the coast although they were a common sight just inland on higher ground. The salt pans on the causeway beyond the town was a popular bird spotting area and we have seen egrets and kingfishers there. Better informed 'twitchers' as I believe they are called with binoculars and long lenses are often seen there presumably sighting the rarer species.
Some wildlife make their presence felt in a different way. Coming out of the airport when first arriving on the island I have heard the sound of crickets in the trees in the car park.

A sound so alien to Britain but so Mediterranean to know you have arrived somewhere quite different.

27 In Hospital

Frequent trips to the island over the years have meant we have added visits to hairdressers, dentist, doctor, accountant, notary as well as several official offices and happier visits to galleries for private views and meals in friends homes. Unfortunately, one autumn we were to add the local hospital to these experiences.

I won't describe the medical details but in summary it involved some diagnoses to correct misdiagnosis back in Sussex and a serious operation. As with most experiences that we have on the island it was a mixture of generosity, humour and strangeness. We were met with kindness and given patient explanations in our language about the diagnosis and treatment options. This was all despite some limitations clearly visible to us in terms of modern equipment and facilities in the country. The care was really good of a high standard but the experience was very different. We both felt that S. felt very safe and well cared for. I will just describe a few of the experiences.

Although food was supplied to the patients and also offered occasionally to visitors as well but the preference for some patients was to bring in hot dishes of food from the local eateries or even, as we witnessed on more than one occasion, for a moped delivery of pitta gyros or pizza with the helmeted rider arriving on the ward! The balcony outside was also used for patients smoking requirements.

Visiting was more relaxed with no apparent restriction on time or numbers, in fact sometimes it looked as if visitors took to touring the wards to check if any other acquaintances were under treatment once they had made their primary visit.

S, benefited from this practice. She received unannounced visits from Maria from the supermarket visiting her uncle suffering a tree climbing related accident and Poppy and Aris from a local restaurant, after they heard she was a patient and their planned visit to a relative was over. It was all very sociable. We were both invited to join in a Greek game of Pictionary by the relatives of a young girl on the ward admitted for an operation.They had obviously over estimated our Greek language prowess, we declined the offer but we did discover

that the family ran a restaurant that we had used some miles
way in a south coast village so received an invite go for a meal
in the future to celebrate a mutual healthy recovery.
Medical attention was different. There appeared to be no
regular doctor's round with a posse of white coated students
who discussed the patient in an abstract impersonal manner in
their presence something we have experienced in the UK. Here
the surgeons would usually arrive alone and sit on the bed and
chat naturally, it was very refreshing. Once when leaving to get
something from the shop Dr Stephan bumped into me in the
corridor and walking with me with his arm on my shoulder he
said "Tell me - how is our girl feeling today? - a positive
attitude is so important for recovery, she is doing well."
We were met with such kindness and skill it made for a positive
experience at a very scary time.
Interacting with other patients was also interesting. Patients
and visitors younger than ourselves normally spoke some
English and some were fluent so our limited Greek was not
essential. Older patients and their family often limited their
conversation to Greek which was fair enough. One visitor a
gentleman of advanced years who sat next to his wife who
seemed mostly sedated showed an interest in our Ipad that I
had brought in to show S. emails and news at home. His
curiosity got the better of him so I explained as best I could
that it was a small television. We were surprised one evening
when he took a break from his bedside vigil to join us on the
sofa in the visitors lounge. We had just watching an episode of
the comedy show 'Black Books' with Dylan Moran, Bill Bailey
and Tamsin Greig. He appeared to enjoy it and at the end we
exchanged names but like many Greeks he struggled with
'Geoff.' In later days he confused S. by asking where George
was which was the name he had given me - I concluded
perhaps unkindly he was interested in my return to catch up on
some more television.
Another strange event happened when I was visiting near the
end of S's stay when we struck up conversation with a lady in a
white coat who came into the small ward and asked if today
was the 'release day.' We were waiting to hear so couldn't
answer fully but assured her that the treatment had been so
good and everyone had been so kind and reassuring. The lady

elaborated on the financing of the Greek health system and entered into a long dialogue on the whole issue of the country public finances and the relationship with the EU in Brussels comparing the position of Greece with the history of the UK and its love hate relationship with the EU project. I assumed she must be a consultant or someone in a hospital managerial capacity so asked her how long she had worked there as a doctor. She laughed and said, "No, I am not a doctor - I am an orderly and have come in to disinfect the bed when patient leaves."

You live and learn.

Upon my first trip to the hospital shop for essentials of water and wet-wipes etc. I was pleasantly surprised to find a well stocked fridge, including lager and beer, supported behind the counter by a full set of spirit optics and this was at 10 p.m. at night! There was food in the hospital but patients seemed to supplement this by bringing food in from home.

After the diagnosis we met with the surgeon in his shared office. He introduced himself as Doctor Stefan, in perfect English and described the necessary surgery but explained S. would need a couple of weeks to gain strength before the op and assumed we would return to the UK for the actual operation. We asked if it was possible to have the operation in Crete. He initially expressed surprise and asked if the facilities would be better for us at home - "the NHS has a good reputation." 'Yes, but on at least two occasions they had failed to correctly diagnose the condition leading to what we now realised was a life threatening condition requiring surgery. Can the operation be done in the hospital here?'

'Yes, of course - it is routine surgery now we know the condition but you know nursing arrangements and post op recuperation facilities are more limited here and the basic facilities are less modern. But yes we can do the surgery - let me see." With that he looked at his Iphone and suggested a date some twenty days ahead and apologised it was so far ahead but would help with the strengthening and he wanted to be on- site for the week after the operation and that was not possible earlier as he had some appointments on the Greek mainland in Athens. He then offered his number for us to call if we had any questions. I offered him our mobile numbers but he said he wouldn't need them.

I explained in the UK operations in hospitals were often postponed if a bed wasn't available or other reasons.

'How odd, only you or I can change the date here' I could see he was rapidly reassessing his opinion of our NHS service.

We used the short wait for treatment to build up S's strength following some helpful pre-op dietary advice from Dr Stephan all given in a thoughtful, kind and sensitive way. We even managed a break in a hotel further to the east on the island. Sitia was a town we had always enjoyed visiting but day trips meant an early start if the shops were to be browsed in a leisurely fashion before they closed early in the afternoon. The restriction was compounded by my need to sit quietly with a calming cold coffee and a cake after the winding route with deep drops in places at the side of the road. One time after taking an abortive turning up a side road to park in a hill village for a drinks stop my loyal navigator abandoned ship announcing she would be able to phone for an ambulance should my ambitious three point turn above a steep drop turn out badly. I was not entirely convinced of the alibi as her handbag with her phone in it had been left in the car in the rushed evacuation!

It made a change to be in the town in the late afternoon and evening with the town streets and cafes full of local people coming out after work. It was close to the end of the tourist season so we had the hotel almost to ourselves. One of the staff explained that they had unusually remained open into November for the staff to have language lessons and although their English was perfect they were learning Italian to develop new business with Italian tour companies.

"Did we speak Italian?" We both answered in the negative although I knew S had spent some time in Italy a while ago. I also felt reviving my schoolboy Latin of some forty plus years earlier would be a strain on what was planned as a relaxing break. The hotel was great, right on the seafront built around a leafy courtyard with an outside pool in it at a quite bracing temperature, in fact I found the sea was warmer. The food was good and the friendly staff had time to chat telling us about the town. We learnt that the harbour used to run a ferry service to other parts of the island and I wistfully thought that would have been a more relaxing way to travel.

Almost three weeks later found us back at the hospital for an afternoon of assessments before the operation the following morning. After these which seemed very thorough we were shown to a small room with three beds in it and an adjoining bathroom as well as an outside balcony. Only one of the beds were occupied with a sleeping lady who had an elderly gentleman sitting in a chair alongside her, we exchanged nods. Once S. was settled in bed I went down to the hospital shop to buy some bottled water and to resist the allure of the beer and spirits on offer. A nurse came in to bring S a light meal so we asked her what time I should leave and whether there were set visitor times the next day. After asking how far I had to travel - (some twenty minutes by car to the next town) to my surprise I was offered a bed for the night in the third bed in the ward - "it will be a comfort for your wife before her operation in the morning and you can go home for breakfast and return to see her in the afternoon after the operation." So I too was to spend my first night in a Greek hospital bed.

After the operation there was a period of recuperation both in the hospital and back in the village house. All told it extended our stay to over two months and we were able to witness the gradual winding down of tourist businesses in the town. Familiar businesses closed for the winter with the family owners harvesting their olive crops or just relaxing and recovering from the seven days a week summer season. We bumped into cafe and restaurant owners in each others cafes using those that remained open. The tour boats were laid up for the season and despite the temperature still seeming akin to a British summer day, at least in day time, locals were adopting warm jackets, hiking boots and wooly hats. This was noticeable when having a pre breakfast swim on the last day of November in the sea in what I judged a comfortable water temperature the sight was met by two passing young bearded guys in puffer jackets and hats walking their dogs with shaking of their heads and an overheard comment of 'English!.'

The direct flights home had stopped so the return was made through a connecting flight via Athens. Quite an experience all in all.

28 'Fringe Benefits'

Buying the house led onto a number of other benefits for us. I had mused earlier that life rarely turns out the way that you expect and that a good maxim is to go with the flow and explore the new unexpected opportunities as they occur.
In 'Small House in Crete' I described our enrolment at home in Sussex in a Greek school for weekly classes in an attempt to at least acquire some greek language skills. The most beneficial part of this was being thrown into a Greek environment for the two hour class which was the usual southern European form of organised chaos. Pupils and their parents as the majority of the class were children, would arrive and depart at random times in the two hour lesson slot. The classes were held in the church hall attached to a Victorian church now converted by the Cypriot community to a Greek orthodox church, complete with icons and incense burners so there were also the occasional appearances of the Greek orthodox priest who would bless the class at the start and end of term and also appear on saint or name days. This was usually accompanied by the sprinkling of holy water using the traditional bunches of basil sprigs. Not a welcome ordeal for some of the teenage girls who had already prepared for the weekend with routines of hair washing and straightening. Initially the lesson were provided by one of the church elders, Mr Bouras, and the textbooks used were Greek junior school books of a 'Janet and John' genre. The children in the stories were supplemented by Disney characters so we found ourselves learning to read, write and speak, "Goofy would like to play bat and ball." Not really the vocabulary that I could see being useful. Now if Goofy wants to buy a full tank of unleaded for his hire car we may be making progress. That would probably be covered in later lesson. Classes in the years following the first one were taken by Greek students who the Greek Ministry of Culture would pay for and it allowed them to earn money whilst studying. The three that taught us over the years were all mature students in their thirties and qualified teachers. Mr Bouras was rather territorial over the teaching and insisted that they spend a number of weeks 'observing his teaching before being allowed to 'teach solo' which must have been somewhat frustrating for them. Eventually they took over

117

although I quite liked Mr Bouras teaching us as we used to have lengthy digressions over the origins of Greek words and their incorporation into the English language. I genuinely found this helped me to remember the vocabulary although the other students enjoyed catching up on gossip whilst this took place. It also put off the dreaded marking of the homework - yes we had homework set!

Attendance at Greek school led to other social benefits. The school was in church close to the Sussex coast in St Leonards on Sea, next to Hastings. The school was on a Friday night at five o'clock, not exactly the best time for almost an hour's journey across Sussex so we planned to arrive early and got into the habit of a strong Italian coffee in a family run Italian restaurant, appropriately named Fortes. Coupled with the Greek class this gave us a weekly fix of Southern European hospitality as the restaurant was owned and run by three Italian brothers around our own age and their sister along with a couple of younger members of staff. Tony and David were front of house while Mario ran the kitchen with some staff. The older sister Lucia worked part-time chatting with customers and ensuring the 'boys' ran things properly. Over the years despite mostly buying just two coffees with a more occasional snack we seem to have become favoured customers and were both welcomed with kisses on both cheeks on arrival and departure. The food was particularly authentic and when in town and not rushing to a class we treated ourselves to one of their delicious pizza or pasta dishes. Conversation in the kitchen was generally conducted in Italian and many a time we speculated that Italian sounded more lyrical than greek and pondered whether it would have been an easier linguistic task for us, but of course our village house was on a greek Island so as they say 'Ti na kanoume' - what can you do.

We discovered that the family came from near Pisa and still owned a family house there and annually returned there for a holiday where other roles were allocated with David shopping, Tony on maintenance and Mario in the kitchen - again! I guess Lucia still organised them.

The Greek church was the scene of both happy and sad occasions. The barbecues were legendary with great slabs of lamb cooked over large charcoal fired trays none of your modern wimpy gas fired contraptions! These were accompanied by huge bowls of greek salad and warm flat breads along with jugs of greek wine.

When the teacher left there was always the doubt whether the Greek Culture Ministry would allocate another teacher and what they would be like but Eleni and Antigone were both great and for the last few years we were taught by George. He was another qualified teacher but also studying at the Royal College of Art and who we got to know best and were pleased to be invited to several of his exhibitions as guests. All the 'student' teachers travelled down from London for the lesson, not the easiest commute on the tortuous Hastings line.

Sadly, Mr Bouras passed away and many of the class attended his funeral which was the first Greek Orthodox funeral we had attended. It was a sad occasion but led to a lighter moment when as a group we planted a tree in the church grounds in his memory before one of the lessons. As the hole was being filled in round the tree by George a small quantity of 'fish, blood and bone' fertiliser was sprinkled around the trunk. One of the younger class pupils whispered to her sister 'I thought he would have had more ashes, he was a big man.'

Her mother swiftly corrected the misunderstanding but the adults knew that Mr Bouras would have been amused.

The other unexpected bonus from the Greek class was my re-entry into the art world which I had left around the age of fifteen when choosing GCE O level subjects. On the drive home after Greek school we passed a double fronted ground floor gallery that always looked busy with a crowd of people chatting holding wine glasses and we recognised that it must be a private view evening but were intrigued that it seemed to be a weekly event. One week our curiosity got the better of us and we called in. That evening I could tell the framed art on the wall was the work of several different artists and through the crowded room we made our way to the reception desk where we were welcomed and asked to sign in to be put on their mailing list and given a form to sign up to become members of what we discovered was the 'Hastings Arts Forum.' We could be guests for that evening and were encouraged to help ourselves to a glass of wine each provided by the exhibitors. This all seemed very hospitable. As we looked at the art on the walls through the crowded room a smiling man asked us if we liked the work in what I easily recognised was a Scottish accent. We said we did and asked if any of it was his work and when he modestly showed us some beautiful coloured portraits that he described as mono prints, a term I was unfamiliar with but was known to S. her education and background having followed a much more artistic path than I had. My enquiry to George, as we were to discover he was called, whether he had always been a professional artist was met with laughter - "Oh no, I had a career in IT - I only started this a couple of years ago. A number of us here attend a weekly print class here at Hastings College. Come along this Friday, I'll arrange for you to see what we do and later perhaps arrange a trial free session - it's very relaxed." I looked again at the rich colours of the framed art and George's smiling face and thought why not.

Friday found me a little less confident as I drove to Hastings but George was very friendly and what did I have to lose, I could always say it wasn't for me.

The Art College was just above the seafront housed in what seemed to be the basement of a Victorian building, although once inside there was natural light to towards the sea where the ground sloped down. There were some dozen 'artists' of mixed ages and George welcomed me wearing a paint stained apron saying it's best not to dress up for printing. He introduced me to the tutor and then gave me a tour of the studio. There were printing beds for the silk screens, drying racks, rows of tables, a huge light box like a jumbo photocopier and a wet-room for spray cleaning the screens. He explained the process for producing silk screen prints from photos which was a technique that interested me more than mono printing which looks to be a more skilful technique and explained that Ian the tutor would explain what I would need for next week to produce my own image. After an initial trial session I signed up for the full term a couple of weeks later. A few months later I had sold the first two limited edition prints at an event in a restaurant in Lewes and within a year I had joined a group of several other printers for the first group exhibition. To our relief we all sold work and it more than recovered the large wine bill that made for a memorable evening. My work was mostly using photographs taken in Sussex and Crete and digitally working on them on a Mac before creating the image sets to transfer to screens. Images photographed in the villages on the island comprised some of my early prints with doors and windows offering easy photogenic subjects.

I enjoyed the mix of creating hand printed silkscreen from digital photos. I also tried some etching and mono printing but wasn't ever truly satisfied with the results. I carried on printing for several more years at the college and made some great friends there. All arising from stopping in a gallery one night. So many thanks George for inspiring me, your art is still more accomplished than mine is but it's not a competition. I was very grateful to tutors Ian, Myles and Jackie as well as learning from other colleagues on the course especially George Mundell, Del Querns and Andy Smith who is a successful and well known commercial artist and printer.

Contact there led to another new experience when fellow printer Del set up a new business with his business partner Richard - a record shop and who of my generation hasn't wanted to work in a record shop! I recommend 'Music's Not Dead' to music fans. At that time Del and Rich had taken a lease on a premises in Bexhill town that was previously a cafe. They were going for a cheap and cheerful makeover before an early opening to sell cd's and vinyl. I offered to help and a week of cleaning and painting followed before a carpenter came in to create the shelving racks and a counter. After the opening I spent the odd day serving there to help out when Rich was off. It was an interesting experience and great to reminisce with customers about favourite albums and bands we had seen. Many customers were buying back catalogue items and it was amusing to see awe struck younger customers reaction to hearing that you had seen the Doors or Hendrix live. A nice nostalgic experience - though hard work I am sure as a business. The business has developed, extending the range of vinyl and putting on live events as well as a mail order business. It has become a destination for musos from all over the south of England and further. The shop has since moved into the Art Deco seafront De la Warr pavilion making it, I would contend, the only grade 1 listed record shop in existence. As a result of our house move I can only visit occasionally and my several Saturdays working in the music business are just another happy memory.

The other avenue that the house in Crete opened up to me was what is happening here on the page. We spend a lifetime writing as students, correspondents by letter and latterly by emails and text. Some of us also apply this skill in our work to a greater or lesser extent but it's common for people to muse - 'I could wrote a book on that.' The experience of finding, buying and renovating the house in Crete made me think that I had material that was interesting enough to write down and just maybe others would find the content interesting enough to read. Advances in desk top publishing and the use of the internet to publish, market and distribute have all made this possible.

29 Travel

Owning a house in another country gave us some unique experiences but we had always promised ourselves that the ownership should not restrict ourselves from travel to other destinations. This seems idyllic as I am writing this with the latest Covid virus restrictions not allowing us to travel outside our city area let alone fly to other countries. Writing about our life in Crete has been helpful therapy during this time which though restrictive for us I acknowledge we are so much better off than many with their worries about necessary exposure to the virus through their work or other responsibilities. It has also been time to reflect on the rich experiences travel to other locations have provided us with some reminders of this surrounding me at home in these housebound times. Our breaks away as part of the comfortable, time rich, Easyjet generation has allowed us to break up the year with trips, usually city breaks to places that previously were viewed through the screen or magazine articles. In recent years visits to Scandinavian countries as well as southern European destinations have provided inspiration for art and interior design projects at home. In the same way that our time in Crete has led to subsequent artistic outputs to be pursued once we are at home with the time in the place spent on soaking up the inspiration to be drawn on at a later date. This approach has been used by us in Portugal, Rome, Copenhagen Stockholm, Helsinki and the Baltic states as well as other destinations. Around the house here I see prints and artworks based on scenes far away. I look at Danish glassware and china, Baltic fabrics, Danish stereo systems from eBay after seeing them in the Copenhagen design museum, clothing from Portugal, a Greek lampshade, a wooly winter hat bought on cold evening in Rome, a waterproof rucksack from Helsinki with matching anoraks, useful in the Welsh winter or summer! They say travel broadens the mind, (and often the waistline judging by some of the great meals we have enjoyed when away) but it also helps appreciate what is at home. City breaks have become particularly popular with us- it's a mix of great facilities with new chances of eating, culture and sightseeing particularly architecture and often city parks have more variety than the countryside especially if you are enjoying it on foot. The differences you notice in other countries and cultures contrast with your knowledge of your own environments and behaviours you naturally expect. I clearly recall the first time I noticed teenagers riding past a church in Crete and the rider and passenger both crossing themselves. It struck as so unusual to my own eyes. These observations are temporarily denied during the current pandemic and it is my hope that the exposure to other cultures and experiences through travel is only temporary as it enriches our lives and often serves to correctly challenge our own beliefs and behaviour.

I have already mentioned that by using the small house as a holiday home we predominantly eat our evening meals out, also it would be a rare day that we haven't stopped in one of the local cafes or bars for an iced coffee or a cool drink. Whether it's the warmer climate, the fact that the town is a holiday resort or sheer indolence on our own part but these activities are definitely always more time consuming than at home in Britain. In our town most of the establishments are along the coast so there is the luxury of just staring at the changing vista that this provides. If not provided with a sea view then the seating is alongside the road or pavement with entertainment provided by passing traffic or people. This gives the opportunity for friends and acquaintances stop and chat or to join you for whatever refreshments you are having which usually prolongs the stay. The cafe owners and staff usually engage you in conversations and if regulars any exchange of news serves to also pass the time. This is definitely a feature of Mediterranean life that initially feels a little intrusive to the more reserved Northern European character but soon is embraced by most as interesting, charming and normal. Returning to Britain to be served by a disinterested surly student in a British eatery can be dispiriting and has in the past stopped us eating out on initial returns to 'home.' I have speculated that the high ratio of businesses operated by actual owners give a greater level of engagement but this doesn't seem be the whole explanation.

It serves to make people feel so at home at the table that was only stopped at for a coffee to prolong the stay to lunch with drinks, ice creams and more coffees and the use of the cafe as a base whilst different members leave and return on shopping sorties. Whole half days can be pleasantly passed in this fashion!

The other service provided by the owners of popular venues is a sort of unofficial 'Citizens Advice Bureau.' No need to Google the best timber supplier or glazier - just ask the cafe or bar owner. Given the high standard of fittings and frequency of makeovers in many of the cafes they have acquired an expert knowledge of all local suppliers. We have received recommendations of furniture, paint and polish suppliers; translations of official documents; directions to doctors and dentists; resetting of a greek phone back to an English menu as well as many other words of wisdom. We received a gift of two old, traditional style Greek cafe chairs after a furniture makeover at one restaurant - and Dimitri even delivered them!

30 Working

Previous writings may give the impression that we did little work on the house ourselves and in some senses for the original build, a radical renovation. This was certainly true but once we had moved in we were able to have some personal input by way of furnishing and decorating. I described earlier the construction of the kitchen, the making of cupboard doors and the painting of the curved wall in the House Layout chapter. In earlier years we had also painted the wooden ceilings white to lighten the rooms.

The latest improvement appeared a little less straight forward -we would paint the upstairs floor. The painting itself was not the problem rather it was accommodating the furniture and ourselves during the process. The main obstacle was the sofa bed. This was not going to leave the room as it had only been able to arrive in the room through the small french doors on the first floor which was before Ianni had constructed the Juliette balcony. We would need to paint the room in two halves but the first task was to choose the paint and the colour. Over the years we had come to realise that local advice is invaluable and also avoids the ' wise after the event' comments from people who can advise you that you should have used this from there and spoken to them before attempting any endeavour. Two of the restaurants in town had painted wooden floors and we were sure that they were being subjected to a lot more wear and tear than our room would have to endure so advice was sought there. Happily they both recommended the same product from the local builders merchant so that made things easier. A trip there produced a colour chart to be loaned as it was their only one. We settled on a sky blue colour that we felt would add a richness to the room so returning the chart we left with the tin of paint, some new brushes , a bottle of white spirit and instructions to use two coats for a resilient finish and to well ventilate the room. When painting the ceilings in earlier years I remembered how quickly the paint had dried and even in October it was still warm both in the day and through the nights. I concluded, wrongly as it turned out, that the floor paint would also dry quickly. Early the next morning found us on our hands and knees painting one half of the floor with the furniture moved to the other half of the room and a plan to return after lunch to paint the other half. Leaving the small window onto the terrace and the electric hatch open a few inches we went down to the town. Our return after lunch found the house smelling strongly of paint fumes and the paint still a bit tacky.

Painting the other half would have to wait and it seems unlikely we could sleep in the top room that night. I remembered that when we first moved in for a week before the delivery of the sofa bed we slept on an inflatable double mattress and I thought it was still in the cupboard under the stairs. Needs must - the mattress was unearthed from the cupboard and mercifully it was complete with a small rechargeable electric pump to inflate it. This was plugged in and it seemed fine so I left it on recharge to use that night.

By early evening the painted half floor was dry enough to move the furniture back across and before going out for supper we repainted the other half. The 'bed' could be inflated on our return. This seemed the best plan as inflated it would occupy most of the free floorspace on the ground floor.

Our evening out followed a regular pattern: walking down the main street in the village exchanging evening greetings with any neighbours we saw who were often sitting on their terraces or in the street outside and answering enquiries -where were we going? - to town? Enjoy your meal. All very neighbourly. The route to town could be varied by following the main road all the way down with the risk of being run over by errant drivers. Turning off the main road and following the old donkey track of rough cobbles risking a twisted ankle or our favoured route on a winding side road parallel to the main road but through the olive groves.

An evening drink in one of our favourite bars, chats with some acquaintances followed by a meal in one of the town's many excellent restaurants. Some nights we walked back up to the village but more frequently a 5 euro taxi ride from the square was our mode of choice, well we were in a small way supporting local business. Then the walk back through the now silent village with the narrow streets well lit by a generous number of small street lamps but getting near our house our part of the village was not so silent. We were greeted at the bottom of the broad steps down to our street by our next door neighbour - Freddy the dog, (known to us as 'No Sex Freddy' after his owner's instruction to him when he frequently and energetically attempted a 'leg hump.') His owner and our neighbour often went out leaving him tied up outside on the terrace, provided with water and his bed and it was normally fine but tonight Freddy had broken free!

He seemed distressed by his newly won freedom but would not let us catch hold of him or his collar. To make matters worse he had a partner in crime, one of the village cats, Jazzy, who normally sat near our house when we stayed there. She was one of the tamer of the local cats and usually pretty affable but whether it was Freddy's distress or some maternal instinct she had taken on the task of defending Freddy and that included against us. It took some ten minutes of coaxing and the bribe of some food to capture Freddy who was now shivering with fear. S. sat outside with him on her lap while his feline protector sat next to them. I went into the house and inflated the mattress but the noise of the pump didn't help the mood of the refugee - still we had to sleep that night although the paint fumes could act as anaesthetic - windows or the roof hatch would need to be left open and what do we do about Freddy? Bringing him inside to a house which had the ground floor space occupied with a blow up mattress certainly seemed insane particularly as his cat protector was reluctant to be separated from him. It was getting late so we sat in the street for a while with a calming nightcap hoping his owner would return soon. Thankfully, she did and Freddy was pacified. We spent a fitful night's sleep on the mattress - movement by one or other of us threatened to propel the other out of bed but it was certainly calmer without Freddy or the cat!

The next morning we surveyed the paint. It would benefit from another coat but we didn't fancy another disturbed night and what if Freddy has mastered escapology. It was early October surely some of the smaller hotels or apartments had vacancies. The first couple of enquiries drew a blank, we wanted to stay nearby so we could paint the two halves of the floor on consecutive mornings. Whilst sitting in a seafront cafe we looked across the bay beyond the causeway where a friend ran a small apartment development with its own cafe that we often visit. Let's try Leda maybe she has some vacancies.

We had the usual friendly welcome ten minutes later when we arrived at the Island Villas. "Yes, we have a couple of rooms this week - it's reaching the end of the season. When were you planning you decorating?" I explained we were in the middle of decorating and remembering our little house from a visit to it when we first moved in she agreed floor painting would be problematic and a juggling act in the space. We were shown the room which in truth was a lovely two storey villa and twice the floor area of our house. A 'friends rate' two night stay was agreed to start that evening. As so often happens in Crete things are sorted out - 'no problem!'

Late afternoon found us sitting on the balcony of the villa enjoying an iced coffee and the view across the bay towards our hill village. Through binoculars we could actually spot the front wall of our house, we were on a holiday away from our holiday home. Dinner that evening was arranged at the only other business on the isthmus a restaurant under the stars next to the canal into the lagoon. A seafood supper with chilled white wine helped us feel on holiday although early tomorrow more painting was planned back at the house to ensure maximum drying time. Going back to the car some neighbours asked how the painting was going, wasn't it smelly in the house? They were amused to hear of our holiday arrangements some two miles away. Kalo taxidi - they wished us with a smile - safe journey. That is perhaps a poignant note to end on in a year when travel worldwide has been restricted and everyone's worlds has paradoxically become smaller because of the interconnection of the modern world and the ease with which the pandemic spread everywhere.

To juxtapose two Dylan quotes - "I Shall be Released" after "Shelter from the Storm."

Printed in Great Britain
by Amazon

81415647R00077